Life Coaching - Life Changing

How to use The Law of Attraction to Make Positive Changes in Your Life

Life Coaching - Life Changing

How to use The Law of Attraction
to Make Positive Changes in Your Life

Melanie Chan

BOOKS

Winchester, UK
Washington, USA

First published by O-Books, 2012
O-Books is an imprint of John Hunt Publishing Ltd., Laurel House, Station Approach,
Alresford, Hants, SO24 9JH, UK
office1@o-books.net
www.o-books.com

For distributor details and how to order please visit the 'Ordering' section on our website.

Text copyright: Melanie Chan 2011

ISBN: 978 1 84694 666 0

A CIP catalogue record for this book is available from the British Library.

Design: Lee Nash

Printed in the UK by CPI Antony Rowe
Printed and bound in the USA by Edwards Brothers Malloy

We operate a distinctive and ethical publishing philosophy in all
areas of our business, from our global network of authors to
production and worldwide distribution.

CONTENTS

This book is dedicated to Michael, with love.

Acknowledgements

Thanks go to the many people who have helped me during my journey through life. First of all I would like to thank my husband Michael for his enthusiastic support and constant encouragement to explore the ideas presented in this book. I have also greatly benefited from the loving support of family, friends, teachers and work colleagues over the years. Special thanks go to Sue Parkin for kindly reviewing the manuscript and providing useful feedback on how to improve it. My own work has also benefited from reading the work of many inspirational writers including Deepak Chopra MD, Louise L. Hay, Susan Jeffers PhD and Julia Cameron.

Preface

For many years I did not realize that it was possible to choose how to respond to situations in life. Instead I often felt like a victim of circumstances, which did not produce good experiences. During the course of my exploration into different ways of living, I came across books that were incredibly inspirational but often made outlandish claims such about transforming your life forever, or instantly obtaining everything that you want. In writing this book, however, I wanted to emphasize the practical, realistic and achievable ways of making changes to your life. I have also attempted to offer some inspirational features in the book through real life examples of how people have used the tools in this book to make positive changes in their lives. Any errors, inconsistencies or omissions in the book are entirely my own.

Introduction

You are now beginning an amazing journey towards a more fulfilling and enjoyable life. The growing interest in the law of attraction through the books and audio-visual products that have been produced in recent years shows that many people want to change their lives for the better and are looking for tools and techniques that can help them achieve this. Sometimes the law of attraction is discussed in relation to metaphysical (or above the physical) thinking and this approach may be particularly appealing to you if you are spiritually inclined. On the other hand, the spiritual based approach may deter you if you are more practically inclined and you would like concrete evidence to back up the claims that are made for the law of attraction.

In recent years life coaching has also become increasingly popular and there are now a range of coaches who specialize in areas such as career coaching, prosperity coaching or relationship coaching. Life coaching tends to concentrate on tried and tested methods of goal setting and action planning which are extremely powerful and effective. This book harnesses both the metaphysical dimensions of the law of attraction and the practical step-by-step processes of coaching in a useful and beneficial way. By using the tools and techniques of the law of attraction and life coaching, as outlined in this book, it is possible to achieve a more fulfilling life.

The three main themes in the book: discovery, clarity and adventure offer a way of becoming more aware of your thoughts, feelings and behaviors. Without awareness you could be living as if you are on automatic pilot, sleepwalking through life. You may also find yourself simply reacting to your moods instead of exploring a range of possible responses to your experiences. Increasing awareness is an important step towards developing the ability to make positive changes in your life.

2

Throughout the book you will be guided through developing effective ways of thinking, feeling and behaving so that you are able to make positive changes in your life. You will also be encouraged to consider a number of factors when making changes in your life, including your beliefs, values and how such changes will impact upon others and the world at large. Raising your awareness and exploring your thoughts, feelings and behaviors will help you to realize how you attract certain experiences into your life.

You will also learn how to clarify what is currently going well in your life and those areas that could be improved. After clarifying the changes you want to make you will be ready to start making plans to make those changes possible. By learning how to set goals effectively you will be able to achieve the changes you want to make in your life. So think of this book as an adventure to a more fulfilling and joyful life.

A word about language

Words such as could, might, or may appear frequently throughout this book for a reason. These words indicate possibility thinking; for some readers this appears to be uncertain or weak language, but for others it points to open-ended thinking. The use of language in this book will become clearer in the chapter that shows how words and phrases can either draw positive or negative experiences to us. The purpose of focusing on language is not to severely monitor every word you speak or write; rather it allows you to consider the sorts of feelings and behaviors that result from them. By regularly practicing the use of positive words and phrases you will start to notice that you are creating more positive and enhancing experiences in your life.

Positive and negative

Some people think that having a positive view of life is unrealistic or even naïve. So to begin with it is necessary to address doubts about the believability or practicality of positive thinking and how this relates to making changes in your life. Firstly positive thinking is not simply accepting every thought, feeling and behavior without question. Instead it is more appropriate to ask yourself if this thought, feeling or behavioral response is supportive or harmful to either myself or to others. Secondly, what sorts of experiences are these thoughts, feelings and behaviors likely to attract into my life?

It is both acceptable and appropriate to think sad thoughts when you lose someone or something that is valuable to you. Simply masking the loss with false positive thinking can be more harmful than good since it blocks the expression of what you are really thinking and feeling. When you are grieving this is an appropriate response to loss. On the other hand, if you become stuck in grief on a long-term basis and are unable to move on then this may be due to unhelpful ways of thinking, feeling and behaving. For instance, you might be thinking that you will never get over this loss and that you cannot cope with life on your own. You might even stop going out or reaching out to others for friendship. Instead of attempting to be positive at all times use words and phrases that are the most appropriate to you depending on your circumstances.

Positive and negative can be thought of as mutually defining rather than in opposition. For example, the meaning of light comes from its difference to dark. Large is meaningful in relation to small; up is meaningful in relation to down. The Chinese philosophy of Taoism focuses on the movement between two terms and offers a useful way of thinking about positive and negative. Taoism emphasizes the cycles of nature, the ways in which day turns into night, or spring into summer. This is all part of the flowing cycle of change. Your happiness may change to sadness and then at some point sadness passes and you move towards happiness again. By choosing to accept happiness and sadness as part of life we can feel less troubled by the movement between them. However, if you want to be happy at all times and on a permanent basis this means stopping the cycle of change and can result in tension. Although it may be unrealistic to expect to be happy at all times, the strategies presented in this book such as examining your thoughts, feelings and behaviors can be used to enable you to cope more effectively with the ebbs and flows of life.

What is the law of attraction?

The law of attraction has become popular through books such as *The Law of Attraction* (Esther and Jerry Hicks), *The Secret* (Rhonda Byrne) or *Law of Attraction – Getting More of What You Want and Less of What You Don't* by Michael Losier. In some cases the law of attraction has been studied from the perspective of quantum physics as a field of energy and vibrations. In other cases it has been associated with metaphysics or the spiritual realm.

It is not necessary to understand quantum physics or practice a particular form of spirituality in order to make the law of attraction work in your life. A useful interpretation of the law of attraction is that it relates to the ways in which we draw experiences to us by our thinking, feeling and behaving. Our thoughts influence our moods, feelings, behavior and interaction with others. You may be extremely good at noticing whether you are sad, happy, irritable or restless. Yet you may not know how these feelings are connected to what you are thinking. So during this book you will be introduced to the tools and techniques that can be used to develop the thoughts, feelings and behaviors that are more likely to produce positive experiences in your life.

You may already be able to detect the law of attraction in your life experiences. For example, do you tend to avoid people who complain a lot? Does negative thinking can cast a gloomy cloud in the home, or workplace? Have you experienced walking into a room and sensing the atmosphere within it? Perhaps you know someone who has a smile that lights up the room, or has a knack of making others feel welcome and appreciated.

Spreading Joy in the Workplace

Some time ago, I worked in a large city center office block. Upon my arrival to work Rosie one of the cleaning staff greeted me. Rosie would smile and say good morning in her lovely Irish accent. Rosie sounded cheerful even on cold, grey, winter mornings. She enjoyed her work and could often be heard laughing and singing while she cleaning floors or emptying the rubbish bins. Rosie's optimism provided a great start to the day. Her happiness was attractive; she radiated joy. Rosie's cheerful presence was a wonderful start to the day.

Examples will be provided throughout the book to illustrate how the law of attraction operates and there will be a range of different exercises for you to complete. This allows you to engage with the material presented, to test it out and refine it so that it works well for you. There will also be examples of how people have used the tools and techniques presented in this book to make positive changes in their lives. You will read about people who have lacked self-confidence, worried about changing their careers, attempted to lose weight or found keeping fit a challenge. The names of the people in these examples have been changed to preserve anonymity and client confidentiality yet the essence of their experience remains intact. These stories are used to show you how the law of attraction operates and how using the tools and techniques of life coaching can produce positive changes. Reading these stories may even inspire you to make similar changes in your life.

During the course of this book you will:

- Identify the connections between thinking, feeling and behaving

- Pinpoint how you resist change and learn how to overcome these tendencies
- Clarify the areas of your life you want to change for the better
- Gain insight into how your values and beliefs impact upon your experiences
- Explore the differences between demands, needs and preferences
- Discover how to use positive language effectively
- Develop your ability to set and achieve positive goals
- Move from un-supportive way of life to a more supportive and fulfilled life

Some of the benefits of this process include:

- Challenging the truth of your negative and habitual thoughts, feelings and behaviors
- Developing the ability to pause, reflect and let go of unhelpful thoughts
- Greater clarity about what is really important in your life
- Increasing your understanding of how thoughts and feelings relate to energy levels and how they attract experiences to us
- Letting go of negative beliefs
- Focusing on possibilities and solutions rather than problems
- Knowing that you are resourceful and that you can change your life for the better
- Understanding how to set and achieve goals to bring about long-term, sustainable changes to your life

Creating experiences

A common interpretation of the law of attraction is that we create our own reality. For some people this can be taken to mean that the external world becomes less important than their own, self-created world. Taken to extremes this could lead to a self-centered attitude whereby the only thing that matters is your own thoughts, feelings and behaviors. It can also lead to self-blame, such as the idea that you are attracting bad experiences to yourself. To counter such views, it is worthwhile considering that there are certain things in life that are out of our individual control such as stock market crashes, extreme weather conditions, life threatening illnesses or the death of loved ones. Although we do not have direct control over these things, we do have some flexibility regarding how we interpret them. So while we do not literally create our own reality, we experience reality through the filter of our own life experiences and sensory abilities. One person might regard a stock market crash as a major economic disaster and start to worry about losing their job. Another person might regard the stock market crash as part of the economic cycle of ups and downs. Someone else might see the stock market crash as an opportunity to buy low cost stocks and shares and wait until the market improves and then sell them at a profit. Noticing that there are different ways of interpreting the same event it is possible to question which viewpoint is more likely to draw good experiences to us.

The law of attraction has also come under criticism on the basis that it produces the belief that we must take responsibility for everything that happens to us. So if you become sick this is because you have attracted it to you. However, it is important to take into account other factors that may come into play with major health issues and take the appropriate medical or clinical action to address them. Nonetheless, if you or someone you love is dealing with a major health issue then it will be beneficial to harness some of the tools and techniques presented in this book as a supplement to the conventional medical interventions that are being used. This book is not about uncovering psychological issues such as past family dynamics, relationships or traumatic experiences. If you are experiencing psychological disturbances due to trauma, past family or personal relationships or have an addiction of some kind, then you are advised to seek appropriate professional support from a qualified therapist, counselor or medical practitioner.

Another view of the law of attraction is that you can simply think positive thoughts and sit back and wait for your life to change for the better. While thinking positive thoughts is a great start, action is also needed to make changes in your life. Just sitting around and having a few positive thoughts is not going to produce dramatic changes in your life. Starting to practice using positive words and phrases is a building block to a better life provided that you start to take actions that support them. Even if you start with a few positive thoughts and actions these will soon gain momentum and before long positive thinking and life enhancing actions will become a much larger part of your daily experience.

Altering your mindset will enable you to be open to new possibilities and opportunities. You can then follow up these opportunities to make positive changes in your life. Supporting positive thinking by actions requires a commitment to making changes in your life. When I take on life coaching clients, for example, a commitment is required from the client to make changes in their life. Sometimes a client may want to move away from their current situation yet it soon becomes apparent that they do not have the commitment to make changes to their lives. In such cases it is necessary to question the client to see how we can move forward. If the client is not ready to make changes and commit to them, it is better to suspend the coaching process until the necessary commitment to change is in place. Consequently having a commitment to practicing making changes to the ways in which you think, feel and behave is required to attract positive changes into your life.

If you are skeptical or doubtful about the law of attraction then this can become a self-fulfilling prophecy. Having doubts is likely to attract more confusion and more doubt towards you. It could be that you are skeptical of the spiritual or metaphysical side of the law of attraction because you are a scientific or logically orientated person. If you are scientifically inclined you are more likely to take new ideas on board when they can be firmly established through experimentation. For those of you who prefer a practical approach to making life changes, this book also includes tools and techniques from life coaching and other areas that have been tested out by professionally qualified life coaches, trainers and teachers. There are also other techniques you can do to reduce any doubts you have about the law of attraction. For example, you may want to conduct your own experiments with the law of attraction by keeping a journal to record your thoughts, feelings and behaviors and see what experiences they bring you. Another option is to create a law of attraction group with your friends to offer mutual support and the sharing of experiences.

Life Coaching

There are some similarities between life coaching and the law of attraction. Life coaching is founded on the notion that you are a resourceful person who can bring about positive and productive changes in your life through the ways in which you think, feel and behave. In addition there are a number of life coaching tools and practices such as affirmations and goal setting that can work extremely well when placed within the framework of the law of attraction and this book will show you how to put these into practice.

A common response to challenges in our lives is to seek the advice of other people such as friends and family. One of the potential drawbacks with asking for advice from friends and family is that those who are closest to you might have deep-rooted issues, or feelings about you. Since you have built up a history with your family and friends they may not be able to provide impartial advice. Seeking advice from others can also be a way of avoiding taking responsibility for your own life. You may make changes based on the advice of others; then if things do not work out you can place the blame on them. A life coach, however, can be an impartial sounding board who will listen in a non-judgmental way to your concerns, ambitions, ideas and plans for change.

Throughout the coaching process you will be encouraged to generate a range of options for making changes based on your values, beliefs and what works for you. The chapters in this book are presented in a sequence, taking you step by step through making positive changes. The first step is to uncover how your thoughts, feelings and behaviors are currently operating in your life. Then you will move on to identify the areas of your life you want to change. After you have identified the particular areas you want to improve, such as health, finances, career or relationships, then you can start to challenge negative beliefs. You may want to read the book in its entirety and then go back and focus on particular chapters and exercises. You may also find writing notes in a journal helpful because this can be an effective way of working through some of the exercises. Your journal can also be an important and valuable record of your own ideas and experiences.

Though this book aims to closely follow the process of undertaking a number of life coaching sessions there are some limitations in attempting to recreate coaching through a book. For example, you will not receive personalized feedback from your coach after completing the exercises. So you may find that you will achieve more powerful results by combining the tools, techniques and exercises in this book with sessions with a suitably qualified life coach. Indeed many of my life coaching clients have reported that one of the most effective aspects of the coaching process was to have someone alongside them to support them in making changes in their lives. You might also want to supplement the ideas, tools and techniques presented in this book with other forms of self-development such as taking exercise classes, or seeking guidance from a nutritionist or health professional. Alternatively you might feel inspired to develop a spiritual practice such as meditation or decide to go on a retreat.

Experts and Role Models

As you proceed through the material presented in this book you may want to seek out a suitable expert or role model whom can assist you with making positive changes in your life. Experts are those who are recognized for having experience and skill in a particular area. Perhaps you admire an expert in a certain field and could draw upon their experiences as you make positive changes in your life. You might be interested in starting your own business, for example, and discover that it is possible to obtain a business mentor who is an expert in technology, communications, marketing or finance. You may want to write articles for a magazine and come across a writer who displays great expertise in this area. In my experience experts are often gracious and willing to share their knowledge and experience. From their point of view it could be flattering to be noticed and appreciated for their expertise. As you progress through this book and start to identify the changes you want to make in your life ask yourself if there are experts who could assist you in this process and make plans to approach them.

Similarly role models are a useful means of support when you are making changes in your life. You can look to role models as an example of what can be achieved, or you may admire their skills, knowledge and experience. Make sure that you can trust your role model especially if you confide in them because those who are unsure about their own talents and abilities may regard you as a threat. You could also choose to discretely observe your role model to find out what makes them successful. Role models can be incredibly inspirational but it is not necessary to simply copy them. Instead draw upon the qualities you admire in your role model and rework them, so that they blend with your personality style.

Inspirational Manager

A few years ago, when I worked for a large public sector organization, I had a line manager who became a role model for me. Harry was in his mid-fifties and had built up a great deal of expertise in business. What impressed me was that Harry had a very positive attitude. Harry thought about challenges and opportunities rather than focusing on problems. He also supported his staff and encouraged me to develop my skills, knowledge and experience. In meetings Harry remained committed to his principles and dealt with opposing views in a firm and fair manner. As a result Harry commanded respect in the workplace. Harry was particularly admired for his confidence and ability to stand firm in the face of opposition by finding mutually beneficial ways forward when conflicts arose. I greatly admired Harry yet also realized that we had our differences and that it was not possible to simply mimic his strengths. Instead, after five years of observing Harry, I considered him a role model and learned to focus on challenges, new ways of thinking, feeling and behaviors rather than problems. I also became more willing to learn from others and undertake further training and education. Most importantly I learned to deal with people in a firm and fair manner.

You might want to reflect upon who you admire and why. What qualities does your role model possess? How could you blend these qualities with your own personal style and incorporate them into your life?

Enjoy the process

The process of change is just as important as reaching your desired results. Making positive changes is life-affirming and can be incredibly rewarding and fun at the same time. You can make the exercises in this book enjoyable by using different colored markers to write down your responses to them. You could also stick inspiring images or quotations in your book or in a folder. You could create index cards or sticky notes with positive reminders on them and carry them around with you throughout your day and refer to them on a regular basis. Another option is to stick positive messages on your computer, fridge, or desk. You might also find it helpful to record positive statements or ideas on your mobile phone or other voice recording device so you can listen to them on a frequent basis. These activities are enjoyable and they are also a way of reinforcing the positive changes you are making.

By making a commitment to regularly practice the ideas presented in this book you will be in a much better position to experience positive changes in your life such as improved relationships, new career opportunities, increasing wealth, or better health.

Chapter One

Thoughts, Feelings and Behaviors

In this chapter you will start to uncover the connections between thoughts, feelings and behaviors. There is a large quantity of evidence based on experimentation and academic studies in cognitive science that shows the connections between thoughts, emotions and feelings. Cognitive therapy, for example, is an approach that examines the ways in which thoughts relate to emotions, feelings and behavior. One of the key ideas within cognitive therapy is that thinking produces emotional states within us.

Dr. Aaron Beck developed cognitive therapy while working with depressed patients at the University of Pennsylvania hospital during the 1960s. Beck found that many of his patients were depressed because they had used the same negative thoughts for some time and that these thoughts had become automatic. Beck traced the basic principles of cognitive therapy to Stoicism, a form of Ancient Greek philosophy, which claimed that it is not a person, object or event that disturbs us; rather it is our interpretation of the experience that generates disturbance.

Beck's work on habitual thought patterns helps us explore the ways in which thoughts are related to feelings and behaviors. Criticism and negativity can have a place in our lives if they allow us to consider the ways in which our thoughts, feelings and behaviors are not working effectively. On the other hand if they become an excuse for not doing anything differently or shutting down possibilities then they will not attract positive experiences to us. If you are thinking in a way that is not supporting your best interests then this can lead to unhelpful responses such as feeling:

Down	Lonely	Anxious	Worried	Tense
Irritated	Annoyed	Ashamed	Envious	Overwhelmed
Guilty	Hurt	Critical	Resentful	Jealous

Alternatively more positive and affirming ways of thinking produce emotional responses such as feeling:

Connected	Confident	Capable	Relaxed
Accepting	Resourceful	Calm	Happy
Contented	Appreciative	Joyful	Excited
Energized	Grateful	Peaceful	Worthy

Below are two examples of how the law of attraction relates to thinking, feeling and behaving in our daily lives. The first example shows how negative thoughts, feeling and behaviors attract negative experiences. The second example shows how such negative thoughts, feelings and behaviors could be turned around so that they are more likely to attract positive experiences to you. After contemplating these examples you could think of some of your own.

It is Monday morning and you wake up in a bad mood. You do not want to go to work and are thinking why does the weekend pass so quickly? You might be worried about all the work you have to do and feel like you are on a treadmill. These sorts of thoughts are likely to make you feel irritable, depressed or sad. As you get ready for work you may move around slowly as if there is an invisible weight on your shoulders.

Then your partner gets up and asks you to make the coffee. You reply that it is their turn to make the coffee. Your partner says that they are feeling really tired and would really like you to do it. You may be thinking this is so unfair, why should I have to make the coffee. You start to feel annoyed, even resentful. Perhaps you slam the coffee jar and make a huge sigh so your partner knows just how resentful you are feeling. This leads to an argument and you start to feel even worse because you are now angrier and more upset.

Finally you leave the house and find that the roads are extremely busy. You may think why do I always get stuck in traffic? Stress and frustration might be the accompanying feelings to this thought. You might start to look at your watch every few minutes and time seems to stand still as your car edges slowly forward.

The thoughts and feelings you are having can mount up throughout the day. If you continue to think angry, resentful or sad thoughts it is likely that by the time you arrive home in the evening you are exhausted and dread the possibility of having another argument with your partner.

On the other hand, it is possible to turn these negative thoughts, feelings and behaviors around. There are other ways of approaching the same sort of life experiences. For example, you wake up feeling grateful for sleeping well. You are thankful for another day of life. It's Monday morning and you are raring to go because you think of your job as a way of offering a service to others. You may be excited about a new work project so feel full of energy and optimistic about your day. As you dress for work you might move around with a spring in your step.

When your partner gets up and asks you to make the coffee, you point out that it is their turn. However, you remember that they have been working really hard putting in some long hours at the office in the past few days, so you make them a coffee to help them out. It feels good to be of assistance and your partner responds to your kindness and thanks you.

Finally you leave the house and get stuck in rush hour traffic. You are curious about how long this is likely to last. You realize that while the traffic delay may result in a long journey it can be made more enjoyable by listening to music. You may even start to sing or hum along to the music.

Making a point of choosing positive thoughts, feelings and

behaviors means that you have a rewarding and fulfilling day at work and you look forward to seeing your partner again when you return home.

What can we learn from these two examples? Notice that the events in each case were exactly the same; it is Monday morning, you are asked to make a coffee and you get stuck in traffic. Yet the responses to these events and experiences can be very different. According to the law of attraction negative energy attracts more negative energy and positive energy draws more positive events and experiences to us. Therefore in the first example, the initial negative thoughts about Monday morning cascaded into further negative experiences of anger and frustration. The ways in which you think, feel and behave in response to these events makes all the difference to your life experiences. You may be thinking that the positive experiences in the examples are not realistic. Perhaps you think that making a drink for your partner, even when it is their turn to do so, is unassertive behavior. Of course there are different ways of thinking about these examples. You may make a drink for your partner but remind them that it is their turn to do so next time. Maybe you find the idea that going to work could be enjoyable hard to grasp and if so, then you could begin to consider how your thoughts about work impact upon your experiences. It is common to think of work as a chore rather than a pleasurable experience so we will return to the ideas surrounding work several times during this book. In particular, you will be guided towards other ways of thinking and feeling about work which are more likely to result in positive experiences for you.

Cascading effect

Have you noticed that if you start off feeling grumpy and irritable first thing in the morning this is likely to cascade to other parts of your daily life? Each negative thought attracts more of the same. This can result in a major negative experience, which you may describe as having a bad day. Over the longer term you may come to view yourself in a negative manner, because negativity has become part of your mindset and your sense of identity.

Positive thoughts are more likely to attract positive experiences to us. You may develop the ability to ride the ups and downs of life by adopting flexible thinking habits. You may be more resilient and accept feelings of sadness, when they are appropriate, rather than seeking to deny them or suppress them. Over time this resilience and ability to cope becomes part of your mindset. Other people may also pick up on your thoughts, feelings and behaviors and regard you as a positive person.

Habits

While the two examples of responses to a Monday morning provided some indication of a few moments of daily life, imagine what happens if such thoughts, feelings and behaviors become habitual. What might be the long-term implications of being grumpy and irritable on a regular basis about going to work, your relationship or getting stuck in traffic? Here are a few examples of how habitual negative thoughts, feelings and behavioral patterns could be showing up in your life:

- Low energy levels
- Unhealthy eating habits
- Poor health
- Excessive smoking
- Compulsive shopping or gambling
- Lack of confidence
- Ineffective relationships
- Lack of fulfillment

Here are a few examples of how habitual positive thoughts, feelings and behavioral patterns can manifest in your life:

- High energy levels
- Healthy eating practices
- Vibrant health
- Self-confidence
- Loving relationships
- Lifelong learning
- Sense of fulfillment

Break the habit

Introducing small changes into your daily routine can help you to overcome repetitive ways of thinking, feeling and behaving. Experimenting by doing new things and allowing yourself to be open to different possibilities will attract different experiences to you. Here are a few ideas that you could incorporate into daily life:

- Do you have your favorite mug or cup for your hot drinks? If so, use a different one, or buy a new one.
- Experiment with your food choices. There are many different types of food that you can sample. Are there any exotic fruits or vegetables that you have not tasted?
- Choose a different route to and from work. You could experiment and find out how many different routes you could take.
- Get up half an hour earlier to write your journal, exercise or meditate.
- Listen to different sorts of music; there are many musical styles and periods to choose from: classical, rock, punk, new age, pop, indie, folk, disco, soul, rap, hip hop, rhythm and blues to name just a few.
- Watch a foreign language film with English subtitles
- Introduce new colors into your wardrobe. You could brighten up a dark colored work suit with a brightly-colored scarf or tie.

These are just a few, simple ideas that do not necessarily cost a lot of money. Remember to think of your own ideas, implement them, test them out and reflect upon how they can lead to changes in your thoughts, feelings and behaviors.

Ripples on a pond

When you have negative thoughts, feel bad or behave in ways that do not support your best interests this is likely to ripple out to others. If you wake up feeling grumpy because it is Monday morning and arrive at work feeling irritable and depressed how will this affect your effectiveness at work and your relationships with colleagues? It is probable that your colleagues will be able to pick up the energy vibrations around you since this will be detectable via your tone of voice, the way you stand, sit at your desk and go about your work day. For example, if you are feeling depressed about Monday morning at work your voice may have a flat tone, you may sit hunched over your desk.

On the other hand, if you are enthusiastic about going to work on Monday morning, you may arrive at your workplace and smile and say hello to your colleagues. You have a stride in your step and when you talk about your tasks for the day you sound excited. You connect well with your colleagues, rather than getting lost in your own thoughts and feelings. You are grateful to have an opportunity to be of service to others through your work and feel fulfilled at the end of your working day.

Putting together the habitual and ripple effect is a potent mix so you could find that your habitual thoughts, feelings and behaviors are having a major impact upon your life. In the following chapters you will learn more about the tools and techniques that will allow you to change habitual thoughts, feelings and behavioral patterns so that they work better for you over a long-term basis. You will also learn about how you might attempt to resist or sabotage changing habits due to the pay-offs they are providing in your life.

In this chapter we have examined the ways in which negative thoughts, feelings and behaviors can cascade and gain momentum. This can result in feeling that you are having a bad day, or over the long-term could lead to feelings of dissatisfaction or frustration. Thoughts, feelings and behaviors ripple out to those around us. Do you want to be thought of as a negative person, or do you want to radiate joy and fulfillment? Start to consider the ways in which your thoughts, feelings and behaviors impact upon your close relationships, working relationships and daily experiences. Positive thoughts, feelings and behaviors also gain momentum. Changing the way you think can result in accepting that not all parts of your day will unfold as planned. But by thinking positively you will be able to deal with frustrations and find ways of feeling satisfied and grateful for your life experiences.

Chapter Two

Positive and Negative Thinking Patterns

The principles of the law of attraction are a way of discovering how thought patterns and feelings operate in our lives. Are you tuning into positive or negative patterns? Think of energy patterns as different television stations and your thoughts and choices are like the remote control. Which programs will you tune into, watch repeatedly, or change? For example consider what types of programs might be broadcast on the negative living channel. Perhaps this channel has shows such as on compulsive eating, fear and self-loathing. These programs appear frequently, they are broadcast daily and they can become a familiar part of your life. At the same time that the negative channel is broadcasting programs of doom and gloom, the positive living channel has different sorts of programs that are more uplifting. The positive living channel has programs like abundance and fulfillment or how to experience gratitude. Upon reflection which channel is more likely to attract positive life changes to you?

You may be a person who has a tendency to put yourself down to friends, family or your partner and this is something that has become a habit. This may stem from long-standing thinking patterns based on your childhood experiences. If you were rarely given praise then it may be challenging to think positively or feel good about yourself. Perhaps bad experiences had a payoff because they brought you sympathy and attention. You may even expect to have bad experiences in your life. So if things appear to go wrong for you then you feel justified in having negative thoughts. Alternatively you may feel surprised if something good happens to you. When good comes into your life you may dismiss it as a fluke rather than considering the ways in which you may have attracted this experience to you by your thinking.

Well-regarded psychologists such as Aaron Beck and David Burns have shown how thought patterns impact upon feelings and behaviors. Their work shows that distorted, negative thought patterns are a common experience. What follows is a summary based on their work on distorted thinking patterns. Recognizing how you use such thinking patterns can be the beginning point of change because you will start to realize that there are other ways of thinking, feeling and behaving. Examples of each of these thought patterns are given to help you recognize how you may be using them in your daily life.

Catastrophizing

This is a way of projecting negative thoughts onto future experiences.

- I will be fired if I do not make my sales targets.
- My career is doomed if I do not pass this exam.
- If I miss my train/bus or airplane this will ruin my holiday.
- If I am made redundant, I will be a failure.

Discounting the positive

This is when you do not value your own strengths and abilities.

- I did well in that exam but it was a fluke.
- My business proposal was accepted but I just got lucky.
- You did a favor for a friend, they complement you for it and you shrug it off saying, 'It was nothing.'

Emotional reasoning

You could feel so strongly about something that you think it must be right and discount any evidence that suggests otherwise.

- You feel left out of your team at work, forgetting that you were invited out to lunch twice last week.
- You feel unappreciated by your manager, overlooking the positive feedback you received for your last project.
- You feel taken for granted by your partner, forgetting that they bought you a surprise romantic gift last week.

Labels

This is when you put a label on something or someone, which then limits your experience.

- That café always serves lousy food.
- She's crazy.
- He is greedy.
- He is stupid.
- You are lazy.
- They are worthless.

Magnification or minimization

This thought pattern distorts your experiences by over empha-sizing or minimizing them.

- You have a few pimples and think you are ugly.
- You put on a bit of weight and think you are no longer attractive.
- You have one grey hair and you think you are 'over the hill'.
- You have a small scratch on your kitchen table and think your kitchen décor is ruined.
- You pass all your exams but still think you are not intel-ligent.
- You work really hard on a team project but believe your input was minimal.

Mental filter

This is concentrating on one negative detail instead of the whole picture.

- You did not stop in time at a traffic light and think you are a poor driver.
- You cook a delicious dinner party but worry that the vegetables were undercooked.
- You score 90% on an exam and focus on the 10% that was incorrect.

Mind reading

This is when you assume you know what other people are thinking.

- You think you will not fit in to your new team at work.
- You think your manager dislikes you.
- You think your tutor thinks you're stupid.
- You think that your friend does not like the present you bought them because they do not look happy when they open it.

Overgeneralization

This is making sweeping statements, which distort experiences.

- You feel awkward at a networking event and think you will never be successful in business.
- You got confused about the date of a meeting and think that you are always getting things wrong.
- Your bus or train is late and you conclude that they never come on time.

Personalization

This is when you take things personally and do not consider

other explanations.

- You think your manager is in a bad mood and wonder what you have done wrong.
- Your bus was delayed and you were late for a meeting so you blame yourself for not setting off earlier.
- Your partner slams the door shut and you think they are angry with you.

These distorted thinking patterns are frequently found in daily life and they can become a habit. Sometimes people combine these patterns which can result in destructive rather than constructive thoughts, feelings and behaviors.

Looking for a New Job

I recently met up with a friend has been looking for a new job for six months so I asked her how she was getting on. Aisha replied that she had gotten an interview, a couple of days ago, but this was a fluke because the company concerned was desperate to recruit someone after an employee had left at short notice. Here we have an example of discounting the positive, since Aisha had got an interview, which was a step forward towards her goal of getting a new job. She then said that she didn't think that the interview panel liked her and was not hopeful about the result of her interview. In this case Aisha was mind reading because how could she know for sure that the interview panel didn't like her?

Distorted thinking patterns tend to attract feelings of hopelessness rather than providing the motivation to make changes to improve the situation. If you are having negative thoughts about the future such as applying for another job but thinking you will not be successful, what can you do to obtain a better outcome for yourself? You may take practical steps, such as practicing your interview techniques, revising your résumé, or approaching the prospective employer for more information. In addition supportive self-talk, which focuses on your skills and achievements rather than your lack of confidence, can also be very beneficial in these circumstances.

It is helpful to view your distorted thinking habits as something that can be changed, with gentle and regular practice. You could make the process fun and enjoyable by challenging the ways in which you overgeneralize, mind-read or discount the positive. Practice other ways of thinking about your experiences and notice the different feelings and behaviors this brings about. Here is an example, which illustrates how to turn an experience around by choosing different thoughts, feelings and behaviors. You forget to put on your alarm and sleep longer than usual. As a result of oversleeping you do not have time to complete your usual twenty minute run. You are planning to run a charity race in a couple of months' time, so your morning run is an important part of your training plan. This experience triggers the following distorted thinking patterns:

- I will not be able to take part in this race because I am not fit enough (catastrophizing).
- I'm always sleeping in (overgeneralization).
- Other people who are training for this race are fitter and more dedicated than me (mind-reading).

These thought patterns are likely to attract feelings of frustration or guilt which may jeopardize your fitness plans.

These distorted negative thought patterns can be changed as follows:

- I'm am not lazy, I needed a rest after working so hard yesterday.
- What can I do to avoid oversleeping?

- How can I re-arrange my day to accommodate my fitness plans?
- I am sure that other runners also find it challenging to maintain their fitness plans

The following exercise helps to identify distorted thought patterns and explore other ways of thinking to attract more positive experiences into your life.

Exercise
What sorts of distorted thoughts do you have on a regular basis?

On a scale 1-10 (1=low, 10=highest) how much do you believe these thoughts?

What sorts of feelings arise from these thought patterns?

How often do you think these thoughts (e.g. several times a day, every few days)?

In what sorts of situations do you think this way?

How are these thoughts impacting upon your behavior?

There are a few simple steps that you can take to change your thinking habits. These include: raising your awareness, pausing, reflecting, making choices and letting go.

Raising your awareness
As you start to read the material in this book you will become more aware of how your thinking habits impact upon your feelings and behaviors. Another way of increasing the awareness of your thought patterns is to write daily in your journal. It is not necessary to write pages and pages of material; instead you can experiment and find out what sort of writing practice works for you. Recording your thoughts in writing can be very revealing and after some time you may start to really notice certain thought patterns emerging from your daily entries.

Pausing

Do you send off a quick e-mail response to a query just to get rid of it? Maybe you have regrets about saying the first thing that popped into your head at a meeting? Counting to ten before speaking when angry is a simple technique that works for many people. Yet pausing can be a challenge in our fast-paced world of instant cash and fast food. Developing a knack for pausing instead of instantly reacting will probably take some practice. Yet the practice is worthwhile because pausing before you speak or act can bring wonderful results. Pausing can make our actions even more effective because simply diving into something before thinking can frequently lead to confusion or mixed results.

Reflection

What are the consequences of hurriedly sending out e-mail to a friend or colleague? Has saying the first thing that popped into your head enhanced or damaged some of your relationships? Reflecting on how your thinking impacts upon your feelings and behaviors can be a way of changing them. After pausing you might reflect upon the consequences of your negative thoughts. You can reflect upon your previous experiences to determine whether a particular train of thought is likely to bring life enhancing experiences or not.

Choice

Upon reflection you may choose to think differently. Raising your awareness and taking time to pause before responding also opens up the possibility of experimenting with new ways of thinking, feeling and behaving. You may start to realize that you can choose to think differently to improve your everyday experiences. Instead of hurriedly sending an e-mail to a friend, you might choose to telephone them or arrange to meet them thereby opening up the possibility of an interactive two-way conversation. Rather than saying the first thing that pops into your head when speaking to someone you could politely excuse yourself, walk away. Remember that you can choose a range of different thoughts in response to the experiences you are having.

Letting Go

If you are worrying about the future or regretting past actions you can choose to let them go. There is no need for your old forms of thinking, feeling and behaving to continue in your life. It is possible to let go of habitual thinking patterns, though this may take some practice. Be gentle with yourself; changing patterns that have been a familiar part of your life, for many years, may take time. Regularly practicing new ways of thinking will, however, yield positive results. Over time you will start to notice that you do feel different and that your behaviors have also changed.

Small steps to big changes

It might be a bit of a stretch for you to move from negative to positive thinking, feeling and behaviors because they have become so ingrained in your life. Attempting to make drastic changes might be self-defeating, because you may become anxious or resistant. So start to make small steps towards positive forms of thinking, feeling and behaving and slowly gain momentum. The following story exemplifies some of the disadvantages of making drastic changes in life.

Martin's Story

From a young age Martin enjoyed eating a lot of sweets, cakes and biscuits. Eating sweet food on a daily basis had become a pleasurable habit for Martin. During his mid-thirties, however, Martin found that he was requiring more dental treatment for cavities and was starting to develop a spare tire around his waist due to weight gain. In addition, his father who also had a habit of eating large amounts of sweet food had recently developed diabetes. Martin decided it was time to change. One morning he went through his snack box and packed up all his biscuits, packets of sweets, cakes and fizzy drinks and gave them to his friends. Two days after this clear-out Martin felt great. Four days into these drastic changes to his diet, Martin started to experience flu-like symptoms, he had a throbbing headache, no energy and found it difficult to get out of bed in the morning. Martin realized that this was his body reacting to the drastic reduction in sugar. As a result, Martin began to take things more gently and gradually cut down on his favorite sweet foods. Over several months, Martin successfully switched to more balanced eating habits.

When you begin exercising, you do not start off doing extremely physically demanding postures or routines because this could lead to a serious injury. If you were starting to train for a marathon and had not done this before you would probably not begin with running 15 miles per day. Instead you might have a long-term plan that starts with smaller steps such as running 10 minutes per day and gradually build up your strength and stamina. Similarly when you start to think, feel and behave more positively you can make small steps in the right direction. Once you make smaller steps and start achieving beneficial results you will probably want to make further changes, at a pace that suits you.

You might already have an inkling of how small things can make a big difference in your life. For example, enjoying the occasional chocolate bar or fried food will not necessarily result in weight gain because this may be offset by regular exercise or be part of an overall healthy diet. On the other hand, if you start to form a habit of eating several chocolate bars per day, or eating large amounts of deep-fried food on a daily basis then this could lead to weight gain. If you occasionally stop walking to the local shops and take the car instead this might not make such a big difference to your fitness, petrol consumption or the wear and tear of the car. However, if you repeat this over a number of months this activity will probably start to have a noticeable effect. Alternatively deciding to get off the bus one stop earlier and walking further home each night after work will certainly add up to more exercise over a weekly, monthly and yearly basis. Walking just 5 minutes extra per day mounts up to 35 minutes a week, 2 hours 40 minutes per month and 26 hours 40 minutes per year.

In this chapter you have learned about the power of choice and that it is possible to tune into either the positive or negative living channel. The terms positive and negative have also been explained in more detail to show that grief and sadness are often appropriate responses to certain situations. Additionally moving towards a more positive life has been shown to be a gradual process. By taking small steps, over time, towards positive ways of thinking, feeling and behaving, you can achieve great things. We have also explored the ways in which awareness of your thoughts, feelings and behaviors is the starting point of change. You can start to make choices about how you respond to situations rather than simply reacting to them. Recognize that it may take a while to override existing thought patterns and practice new ways of thinking. Take things gently at first and remember that small steps often lead to big changes.

Chapter Three

Resistance

While you may find it easy to identify the thoughts, feeling and behaviors that are not supporting you, changing them may seem like a tall order. Furthermore, even those habits that are not moving you towards a more fulfilling, healthy and productive life are at some level fulfilling a need. Overeating, for example, can be triggered by negative thoughts about yourself, particularly your body shape. These thoughts are likely to make you feel miserable, so you attempt to feel good by comforting yourself with food. Although overeating provides a temporary sense of comfort, over the long-term this type of thinking, feeling and behavior could become a habit that is detrimental to your health and well-being.

Before delving into making changes in your life it is useful to consider the ways in which you may resist such changes. When changes are the result of external factors you may resist them because they appear to be imposed upon you. At a personal level you may feel powerless because you were not involved in the decisions that brought about these changes. Even if you do instigate changes in your life, there may still be some resistance on your part because you may be unsure about the outcome. You might feel a sense of sadness or loss for what you are giving up. You may, for example, decide to move to a new house. You are thrilled to have a new place to live, or more space, yet at the same time this might be tinged with sadness about leaving your old house and the fond memories you have of living there. You might also miss your former neighbors and the community that you were part of.

Altering unhelpful ways of thinking, feeling and behaving can meet some resistance, for a number of reasons. Even though you want to change, you may think it is difficult to do so because you have become accustomed to thinking, feeling and behaving in a particular way. In other words you have developed a habitual response to experiences and events. If someone criticizes you, for example, your habitual response might be to think that this is unfair or unjustifiable. You may feel angry and upset and behave defensively by speaking unkindly or storming off but this type of response tends to generate more conflict. It is also unlikely that this sort of response will lead to a beneficial experience or an effective solution for either of those involved. When attempting to make changes in your life you may come up with what seems to be perfectly reasonable explanations for not changing after all. Upon closer inspection it is worth asking if these are reasonable explanations, or if they are actually excuses.

Miriam's Story

Miriam was invited to give a presentation at a major, three-day information technology conference. This was an excellent opportunity for her to present her ideas and network with some of the key people in the industry. Miriam was surprised to find that she was feeling anxious about the conference and fearful of standing in front of a large audience and presenting her work. As a result, Miriam made an excuse to the conference organizers and said that she was no longer in a position to attend the event or give a presentation. Miriam found that there were a number of factors contributing to her resistance. Firstly she was worried that the conference presentation would mean a lot of extra work for her and doubted her ability to cope. Secondly she felt that her shy personality was set in stone and that she could not be a confident speaker. Thirdly she was concerned about whether the cost of attending the conference would impact upon her finances. After backing out of the conference Miriam felt a mixture of relief but also frustration at her lack of confidence. Miriam knew that if she continued to think and act in this way that this would impact negatively upon her career prospects. After undergoing several courses on assertiveness, positive thinking and presentation skills Miriam started to change. It took some time to develop her self-confidence but it was well worth the effort. Three years later, Miriam had the confidence to travel alone to an international conference in the United States. She spoke confidently to a large audience and her ideas received positive feedback.

There are many excuses that can be used to resist making changes in our lives. Wayne Dyer provides a particularly insightful and useful way of understanding how we use excuses in his book *Stop The Excuses! How to Change Lifelong Thoughts*. Indeed there are a number of stories we can tell ourselves in order to justify our excuses. One of the most powerful excuses is thinking that changing is going to be difficult or hard work, so why bother? Another excuse is based on the idea that your personality is set in stone and there is nothing you can do to change it. Both of these excuses tend to produce feelings of resignation and it is unlikely that they will produce positive changes in your life.

These two excuses indicate how the principles of the law of attraction operate in common situations. Thoughts such as changes are too much hard work or that you cannot change lead to stagnation and will not draw positive experiences or opportunities to you. If you continue to think, feel and behave in defeatist ways then the law of attraction will bring more of the same into your life. Change will become difficult for you because this is the message you are sending out. Furthermore, there is a pay-off to these excuses because they seem to be a reasonable way of avoiding change. In other words these stories allow you to do nothing and find a way of justifying your lack of action.

There are, however, tools and techniques that can be used to address our resistance to change. In particular, life coaching focuses upon generating options for change. Life coaching is based on the idea that it is not necessary to draw upon habitual responses or excuses anymore. You have the ability to generate a range of options and can make choices that support you. Generating options in this way is also likely to attract new opportunities to you. You may, for example, have a habit of reacting defensively to criticism. You may justify your defensiveness with stories such as you are an extremely sensitive person so this is how you react to criticism. You may think that it will be really difficult, or unrealistic to react in a different way to criticism. One way of overcoming this habit is to briefly pause when you think that you have been criticized. By pausing you allow yourself time to decide how you want to respond and what will be most effective for you. The brief pause is extremely important because it stops the knee-jerk reflex of your habitual responses. It opens up a space of possibilities that allows you to choose from a range of responses instead of just a default response.

Here is an example of how a brief pause can open up a multitude of possible responses for you. A work colleague may accuse you of making too many mistakes in a report. You may think they are in no position to criticize your report. Perhaps you think that they do not appreciate how much effort you put into this report. On the other hand you may be hard on yourself and think that you are not intelligent or experienced enough to write good reports. These sorts of thoughts are likely to make you feel upset, angry and threatened. They may result in behaving defensively, being sarcastic or even storming off. Unfortunately this type of response is likely to attract more conflict. The long-term implications of this type of thinking, feeling and behavior might be poor relationships with your work colleagues, ongoing bitterness and resentment.

Another way of dealing with this experience is to consider

that there may be ways of improving the report that you have not considered before. You might start to see that there could be some truth to the criticism. You might be curious about whether this person has a pattern of criticizing others, or if they are attempting to help you by pointing out areas that could be improved in your work. These sorts of thoughts and feelings are more likely to involve further contact with your colleague. You could ask them what they think you can do to improve the report, or if there is someone else who could help you rewrite it. As a result you and your colleague are exchanging information and ideas that will attract new ways to change or improve the report. Over the long-term you might start to work together harnessing your creativity and ideas, rather than working against each other.

If your colleague is attempting to undermine you and the criticism is unjustified then you still have a range of responses available to you. It may be that you decide to address the situation by stating that you are unsure about the validity of this criticism and ask if there is anything else that is bothering them. You might decide that this is part of an ongoing destructive relationship and seek to be moved to another department, or seek some sort of mediation process. However, when you turn the criticism upon yourself this can lead to self-blame and loss of confidence. If this happens then workshops or training to build up your assertiveness can help the situation. The important thing to note in this example is that there are many ways of dealing with criticism and that some can be more effective than others.

Doubt

Do you doubt that your thoughts, feelings and behaviors draw certain experiences to you? Perhaps the law of attraction seems too metaphysical and you want proof that it works. Doubting can weaken the intention to make changes in your life and become a self-fulfilling process. If you have doubts about the effectiveness of the law of attraction then you are unlikely to make changes to your thoughts, feelings and behaviors. Subsequently this does not open up the possibility of drawing more enhancing experiences into your life. When doubt arises you can ask yourself if this is a form of resistance or if it is your inner wisdom attempting to guide you in a different direction. Recording your thoughts and experiences in your journal can be a way of tracking and becoming aware of these differences. Experiment by recording the results you achieve from making changes to your thinking, feeling and behaving in your journal. You might decide to do some research and find evidence that supports the effectiveness of the law of attraction, life coaching and positive thinking. You may want to question whether this research has credibility; for example, was it part of a well-conducted study? You could also find out how these tools and techniques have worked for other people by writing or joining an on-line discussion group. Finally, keep an open mind because sometimes it is not possible to find cast iron certainty. Studying our thoughts and feelings is not the same as obtaining data or measurements about non-physical objects such as the weight of a rock, or the size of a sheet of paper.

Finance

Financial reasons are frequently used as a means of putting off or avoiding making changes in our lives. You might think that change will involve some sort of sacrifice. Perhaps you are concerned about making financial sacrifices such as reducing your working hours. On the other hand, is continually working overtime costing you in terms of your close relationships with family and friends? Could working extra hours be damaging to your health over the long-term? Do those extra hours actually make your work more effective, or do you find yourself making more mistakes due to fatigue? Then again you might be concerned about paying for self-help books, workshops or life coaching sessions. On the other hand, ask yourself what is the cost of remaining where you are. Paying life coaching fees can be regarded as an investment in yourself because it could be a way of improving your career goals, health, finances or relationships. Self-help books, tapes and DVDs can also be bought second-hand, or swapped with friends, or even borrowed from the public library. On a positive note downsizing to a smaller house could bring many benefits such as saving money on bills. Your property rates may also decrease, or perhaps you will need less furniture.

Mixed messages

When you start to work towards making changes in your life you may become fearful. You may be fearful because you are feeling unsure that you are heading in the right direction, or making the right choices. One part of you may want to change but another part of you could be fearful thereby leading to mixed messages. The law of attraction will not be as effective if you are holding contradictory thoughts about change. This could manifest as feeling as if you are taking one step forward and then one step back. When fears start to develop, your intention to make positive changes in your life becomes split. This can feel like you are pulling in opposing directions. Wanting to change but having fears about change generates tension and wastes energy. Your thoughts start to conflict with one another and this creates confusion. Fearful thoughts and feelings can also lead to withdrawal because you may back away from the changes you were starting to make. Over the long-term such behavior can lead to time wasting and missed opportunities as you squander the opportunities for change that are presented to you.

Rather than denying or suppressing fearful thoughts, feelings and behaviors you could start to explore them in more detail. Fear is not necessarily negative because it enables us to activate our flight or fight response when confronted with danger. On the other hand, if fear prevents us doing something that could be beneficial such as starting a new relationship, or taking up a new job, or moving house then this is not helpful. By exploring your fears you can start to generate a range of options and then choose how you want to progress. If you want a relationship, for example, you could join a dating service and meet a potential romantic partner but then start to feel fearful about relationships. You could then explore whether your fears are justified, or if this is just another excuse for not getting involved in a relationship. You then have a choice; you can move through your fears and trust in yourself, or you could decide to suspend your subscription to the dating service until you are clear about what you want. Alternatively you may decide to date a few different people before deciding if you want a serious, committed relationship.

Helen's Story

Helen decided to take driving lessons which was something that she had put off for years for a number of reasons: fears, insecurity and lack of funds. Despite taking over 90 hours of driving lessons, Helen still had fears about her own abilities. These doubts manifested as thoughts such as "I'll never learn to drive," "Why am I so nervous about driving?" "I'm wasting time and money on these lessons because I am not getting any better at it." Helen's thoughts led to feelings of hopelessness and frustration. In turn these thoughts and feelings attracted undesirable behaviors such as driving too fast due to nervousness or panicking when meeting other traffic. As these fears persisted Helen began to think that maybe she wasn't cut out for driving after all and maybe the best thing to do would be to quit. Helen had mixed feelings about driving; she wanted to learn but also doubted her abilities. Helen did not realize that her thoughts were attracting feelings and behaviors that were not helping her to reach her goal of passing her driving test. Also, Helen was judging herself very harshly by not considering the ways in which other learner drivers may well think similar thoughts about their abilities. By pushing beyond these un-supportive thoughts, feelings and behaviors Helen gained the impetus to continue her driving lessons. Gradually as the negative thoughts subsided, Helen realized that she had actually started to enjoy driving lessons and this led to improvements in her driving skills.

Sabotage

Resistance to change can also take the form of self-sabotage; this occurs when you start to make changes but then start thinking in self-defeating ways. Often self-sabotage is a form of fear. You may be scared about what might happen when you start to make changes in your life. Self-sabotage occurs when you start to behave in self-defeatist ways which takes you further away from what you are seeking to change for the better.

Amir's Story

Amir wanted to start his academic career by building up his publishing profile. Amir submitted several papers to journals and book editors, for consideration, with mixed results. After receiving a number of rejections, Amir began to sabotage his own efforts by doubting his abilities. He started to have self-defeating thoughts such as "I'm not good enough," "No one is interested in my work," and "I don't have the right connections in publishing." As a result of these thoughts Amir began to feel dejected, thinking, "Why bother continuing to submit papers for consideration, it is a waste of time?" This led Amir to self-sabotaging forms of behavior such as avoiding writing and submitting any further pieces of work to publishers. Amir also began to distract himself by surfing the Internet, going out drinking and socializing with friends. After a time, Amir realized that his colleagues were progressing; some of them had also received rejections but they had continued to write and revise their work for publication. Whilst Amir had been putting off writing his colleagues had stuck it out and were now starting to build up their publishing profile. Amir realized that he had sabotaged his own efforts and resolved to write new material and revise his previous work and submit them to publishers for consideration. He also began to explore other ways to publicize his research such as conference papers and public lectures.

Blaming others

Blaming others is another form of resistance to making changes in your life. It may seem easier to blame others for your current life situation rather than take responsibility for them. You may, for example, blame your current lack of finance on your partner's spending habits. You might then use lack of money as a reason for not starting your own business. Or you may blame your lack of career progression on your manager because you think that they have not given you the opportunities you deserve. Blaming your manager in this way could be a way of deflecting attention away from your own lack of initiative. For example, have you actively sought out further development opportunities yourself, such as training or studying for additional professional qualifications? Furthermore, it is possible that you have not discussed the issue of progression with your manager, so that they are not even aware of what sorts of progression opportunities you are interested in. If your manager is aware of your career plans and has not supported you then you could consider other ways of developing your skills, knowledge and experience such as doing volunteer work for community groups or charitable organizations. The following exercise asks you to be honest about how you could be blaming others for your current situation.

Exercise

What are the pay-offs that you are receiving for blaming others?

What are you thinking about when you blame others?

What sorts of feelings does blaming others generate for you?

How do you behave when you blame others?

What other ways could explain your situation?

What would be the best way to feel about your situation?

What could you do to change your behavior and stop blaming others?

What sorts of experiences does blaming others attract into your life?

Blaming circumstances

Blaming external circumstances is similar to blaming others because it is a way of avoiding taking responsibility. Additionally, blaming circumstances can lead to apathy, resignation or feeling defeatist. Perhaps you decide not to cancel a day trip into the country because it is raining. You may think that your plans have been ruined because of the rain, feel frustrated and sulk around the house. Blaming external circumstances in this way is not going to change things for the better. Even so there are ways of turning around your thoughts, feelings and behaviors. You could choose to think it may be raining but it is still possible to enjoy yourself. There could be ways of enjoying your day after all such as:

- Dressing appropriately for the rainy weather. You could put on a raincoat and a pair of boots and make the best of it;
- Decide to spend the time in a country café enjoying home cooked, local specialty food;
- Re-schedule and do something else with your day, visit a museum or gallery;
- Go to an indoor leisure center or a shopping mall;
- Stay at home and watch your favorite movie, or relax by reading a good book;

- Call your friends and ask them to come to dinner at your house.

Similarly it is quite easy to blame external circumstances such as an economic downturn when you are finding it difficult to obtain a job. You might be tempted to think that the economy is in decline and companies are not hiring new staff so it is a waste of time looking for another job. This type of thinking then produces such feelings as sadness, resignation, boredom or even wallowing in self-pity. You may then do nothing to look for another job and just sit at home being miserable. Even though the economic climate might be tough there are still things you can change to make the experience more positive and productive. You could think about what you could do to improve your chances of getting a job. You could start to explore your options such as:

- Deciding to retrain for a different type of job;
- Doing further study to improve your chances of getting a job;
- Brushing up your résumé and interview skills;
- Joining networking groups where you will meet others and find out about opportunities;
- Exploring the possibility of self-employment;
- Volunteering to get experience or a foothold in an organization.

If Only

The term 'if only' usually occurs when you would like circumstances to be different. It can be a way of justifying your current thought patterns, feelings, and behaviors rather than changing. The term also suggests two conflicting patterns; perhaps you want to change yet you believe that something or someone is preventing you from doing so. Here are a few examples of how 'if only' thinking might be showing up in your life:

- If only I was younger then I would travel the world
- If only my partner looked after the children then I could go to evening classes
- If only I had more energy then I could do more exercise
- If only I had more willpower then I would be able to lose weight
- If only my manager was more flexible about working patterns then I would have more work life balance
- If only I had more confidence then I could go out and meet others

Rather than use 'if only' type thinking and waiting for the perfect circumstances to arise, explore what you could do instead, for example:

- What travel options are appropriate for you?
- What learning opportunities will suit your needs?
- What sorts of exercise would suit you?
- What could you do to lose weight?
- What working options does your employer offer?
- What can you do to increase your confidence?

Timing
A frequent form of resistance is the issue of time. You may avoid making changes because the time does not seem to be right, or you may put off making changes until you are forced to do so by external circumstances. A common reason for putting things off is because we are waiting until the ideal conditions arise. Renowned author on positive thinking, Susan Jeffers, has pointed out that this form of time-related resistance can be detected by the phrases 'when/then'. These phrases operate in the following way:

- **When** I am rich **then** I will be happy
- **When** I retire **then** I will get round to doing the things I really want to do
- **When** the weather is better **then** I will start exercising
- **When** the economy improves **then** I will start looking for a job
- **When** I get over the hurt of past relationships **then** I will look for a loving partner
- **When** I finish this project **then** I will spend more time with my loved ones
- **When** I have enough money **then** I will start my own business
- **When** I feel confident enough **then** I will join networking groups
- **When** I feel in the mood **then** I will tidy up the house
- **When** Christmas is over **then** I will stop drinking

You could be waiting a long time for the perfect conditions to arise before taking action, if they ever do. The perfect conditions may not come to pass, so it is important to go ahead with your plans anyway. Waiting until you feel like doing something before starting it can often be just an excuse for putting things off. When you do start to take action you will find that this builds momentum and positive feelings.

Jane's Story
Jane was a visual artist who often experienced creative blocks. When these blocks occurred she would say to herself, "when I feel more creative then I will start painting again." However, this led to feelings of anxiety about when she might feel more creative. It also led her to doubt her creativity, which attracted more anxiety and frustration. Jane found that she was using a lot of energy on worry, doubt and anxiety but this was not bringing her any closer to feeling more creative. She was also

starting to engage in distracted forms of behavior such as watching too much television, or mindlessly surfing the Internet looking for inspiration. Jane decided that her approach was not working and that different tactics were called for. Tidying up her studio one day, Jane came across some old acrylic paints that she had not used for two years and a canvas that she had started but had left unfinished. Jane decided to have some fun with the acrylic paints. She put on her favorite music in the studio and started mixing up some vibrant colors. After applying the colors to the canvas, she saw her unfinished painting starting to develop and began to become immersed in what she was doing. She realized that it was the act of painting itself that generated the feeling of being creative so she did not need to wait until she felt inspired before starting to paint.

Exercise
Reflect upon your own use of the when/then form of thinking.
In your journal or folder write down your own examples of
    using when/then as a form of resistance.
What could you do differently?

Mix and Match
Sometimes resistance can include a mixture of elements such as fear, blaming yourself, blaming others and circumstances. In these cases it is necessary to untangle the different elements and see how they are contributing to your experiences.

Oscar's Story
Oscar was a talented and experienced science teacher who came to England with his partner, who was studying at university. Despite having the required qualifications and experience, Oscar found it challenging to obtain a teaching position – even a temporary one. The situation was frustrating

because Oscar knew that there was a shortage of science teachers in England at the time, so he could not understand why he couldn't find work easily. After having over ten interviews in just a few months, Oscar decided to have some life coaching to improve his interview skills. During coaching, Oscar continued to go to interviews and reflect upon the process. To begin with Oscar lacked confidence and thought that he was not good enough. After thinking this way, Oscar became fearful and anxious about interviews. On one occasion when an interview panel member asked him a question, his mind went blank due to nerves. Oscar's fear also manifested as unsupportive behaviors such as not looking at the interview panel directly, or mumbling responses to questions. Oscar began to put off his job seeking because he thought that when he felt more confident then he would go for further interviews. What happened was that waiting around for confidence to magically appear did not come to pass. Oscar realized that if he went to further interviews this would actually enable him to practice responding to questions and acting more confidently. Nonetheless, after having a few more unsuccessful interviews, Oscar started to sway towards blaming others. He started thinking that the interview panel did not like him, or they were not welcoming, or even fair to him. Blaming of the interview panel then developed into blaming external circumstances. Oscar started to think that he was experiencing racial discrimination at interviews. Through the coaching process we explored a number of options to help Oscar; these including role-playing interviews, body language, developing effective communication techniques, challenging negative beliefs and increasing confidence. As Oscar's confidence developed his motivation soared. He began to be self-supporting rather than self-defeating. It was incredibly rewarding to find out that Oscar soon obtained a permanent teaching job at a well-regarded school.

By completing the exercises in this chapter you will be able to work through your own ways of dealing with resistance. You will find that dealing effectively with resistance will attract more positive opportunities to you. Writing in your journal about your forms of resistance and reflecting upon your experiences can also be incredibly helpful.

Chapter Four

Commitment

Making changes to your thinking, feeling and way of behaving will bring positive changes into your life provided you are willing to practice the tools and techniques in this book. If you are just interested in obtaining information from this book but are not prepared to take any form of practical action then you will not be able to make the most of the tools and techniques that are offered to you. Acquiring information about the law of attraction and life coaching is a good starting point but this needs to be backed up with a commitment to positive change.

At first glance making a commitment to change may seem daunting, even off-putting. Nonetheless making a commitment to the process of change will be incredibly rewarding and your efforts will be rewarded with positive results. Imagine if you took your car to the garage because it needed some essential repairs and your mechanic did not seem committed to fixing the car. Perhaps the mechanic shrugs and seems nonchalant when you attempt to describe the fault with the car, or does not give you a timescale for the completion of the repairs. You would probably think that they were not fully committed to providing a good service to you. As a result you might seek an alternative garage that could provide a better service. What if you paid up front for an expensive, four-day residential training course, but the trainer only turned up to half the sessions? Again you might suspect that the trainer was not committed to providing a good service and would probably seek a refund. Similarly if you are halfhearted about commitment to making positive changes in your life then you will not reap the full benefits of the process.

You may have come across self-help books that make extravagant claims about making dramatic changes in your life. These books tend to provide a great deal of inspiration but in some cases they downplay the time, effort and commitment that are required to make such changes a reality. My experience as a coach has provided me with insight into the importance of making a commitment to change. Some clients, for example, are unhappy or even distressed about their current situation and really want to make changes to improve their lives. Nonetheless when it comes down to actually implementing those changes, through taking actions, they then become resistant and the life coaching process is not as effective as it could be.

Claire's Story

Claire was a young executive who enjoyed her job at a national bank. Recently she had been promoted to a senior position at another branch. She was also in a long-term relationship and had two children and enjoyed spending time with her family. Claire came to life coaching because she was exhausted due to working long hours, travelling to her new workplace and had little time left for her family. Sometimes Claire would work in the office until 7 or 8pm, return home, make supper and then go straight to bed. At other times she worked from home, using her laptop at weekends, while her family was involved in various activities. Overworking was starting to become a way of life for Claire. The long-term result of this way of working was that Claire was worn out. She was not eating properly and her health was starting to decline. Her relationship with her family was also under a lot of strain. After some reflection Claire realized that time management was a major issue for her. In particular Claire found it hard to delegate, or say no to tasks, which left her feeling overcommitted. She took on projects and attended meetings when other members of her team could have done so. As her distress increased, Claire decided to have some life coaching specifically on time management. What happened was that Claire would often schedule a coaching session then cancel it a few hours before it was due to take place, or would arrive considerably late. Furthermore, while Claire enjoyed having a dedicated coach who would listen to her, she was less effective at putting goals into place and taking actions to improve her situation. After three coaching sessions and little progress it became apparent that Claire was not ready to change. As a result, the coaching process was suspended and Claire was invited to return to it when she was ready to do so.

When entering into a coaching relationship with a new client, I begin by exploring roles, responsibilities and commitment to the process. The first life coaching session covers ethical codes of conduct, terms and conditions and the coaching contract. At the end of the first meeting, the client and I sign the coaching contract. We both agree to listen, be non-judgmental and to provide adequate notification of cancellation of meetings. Signing a contract provides evidence for both parties that they are committed to the coaching process. Likewise, the following exercise is a way of demonstrating to yourself that you are committed to making positive changes in your life

Exercise
Complete the following contract confirming your commitment to change. You may want to copy the contract, add color to it, or highlight certain areas. You can also add your own statements of commitments listing those things that are important to you. It may also be useful to display the contract where you will see it on a daily basis. Viewing your contract on a regular basis will help to reinforce your commitment to making changes in your life.

Life Changing Contract

I agree to:

- Take responsibility for taking appropriate and necessary actions to change my life for the better;
- Be self-motivated and committed to the process;
- Start a journal, or folder to record my progress;
- Question unsupportive thinking, feeling and behavioral habits and replace them with more positive ones;
- Be willing to seek other sources of specialized or professional support if required;
- Do the exercises in this book and reflect upon my experiences;
- Take reasonable steps to progress towards my goals.
- Now sign and date your contract.

Perhaps your current situation is dissatisfying but the thought of really committing to change and taking action seems overwhelming. The following options may help you with this process:

- Return to the chapter on resistance and do the exercises that will help you overcome fears, deal with excuses etc;
- Learn more about tools and techniques for change;
- Do some of the exercises in the book and come back to others at a later point;
- Experiment by making small steps, taking action and reflecting on your results;
- Hire a life coach, or undergo counseling to give you additional support when making changes in your life.

Expectations

What do you expect from coaching with the law of attraction? Are you expecting major changes to take place, or would you be satisfied with smaller, incremental changes that slowly bring long-lasting results? The tendency to expect instant results can have a downside. A five-minute loan, for example, can over the long-term result in inflated repayments based on a high rate of interest. Instant cash may tempt you to overspend. Electronic messages can be sent speedily across the world yet they are not necessarily read with care, or responded to in the detail you require.

Do you expect that after reading this book and doing the exercises all your problems will be solved or that you will be positive all the time? This book can certainly help you re-frame problems into solutions and increase the likelihood of feeling positive. Yet it is probably unrealistic to expect to not face any challenges as your life changes and develops in unexpected ways. It is more useful to follow the example of the highly regarded spiritual writer and teacher Louise L. Hay, who says that by thinking positively, doing affirmations and making changes in her life, she is happy about 75-80% of the time. In other words, sometimes she feels more positive than others. Nonetheless over the long-term she has increased her happiness factor to a high level.

It is not necessary to push yourself unnecessarily or to insist that your life must be perfect. You could find that once you start to make small changes for the better, you will start to enjoy the process just as much as the outcomes. If our lives were 100% perfect then we would not have the opportunity to grow, develop and enrich our experiences. Instead of aiming for perfection, start to be open to experimentation. Do the exercises in the book, experiment with them; alter and refine them so that they suit your specific requirements. The following exercise aims to clarify why you want to change and how committed you are to this process.

Exercise

Is there a specific issue that you want to explore, or do you just feel stuck or unsure about things in general?

What sorts of things do you think change might involve?

What are you expecting from this process?

What specific outcomes are you aiming to achieve?

What will happen if you do not take any action, or make any changes?

On a scale of 1= low to 10= high, how committed are you to make changes in your life?

Most of the life coaching clients who have completed the exercise on commitment are willing and excited to start making changes in their lives. Virginia was a client who said that she felt at a 10 in terms of making changes in her life. To begin with she thought it would be realistic to start at an 8 and move upwards. You may also find it worthwhile to return to the issue of commitment as you continue to make changes in your life. For example, some clients find it useful to re-evaluate their commitment to change on a monthly or quarterly basis.

After working through this chapter you will start to realize that when you are fully committed to making positive changes you are more likely to draw the experiences, resources and people towards you who can make this possible. Being inspired is the first step towards changing for the better but this also needs to be backed up with commitment to change. Taking responsibility for change can be incredibly motivating – it puts you in charge of your personal development. Consider the benefits of incremental changes in the right direction rather than quick fixes. Reflect upon your expectations: are they practical and realistic for you? Remember that drawing up and signing your own life changing contract shows that you are committed to making positive changes in your life.

Chapter Five

Needs, Demands and Preferences

Asking questions about your needs and preferences is a way of discovering what motivates and inspires you. At a basic level we need air, clean water, food and shelter. Yet there are many different ways of meeting these needs. Vegetarians choose non-animal sources of protein such as fruit, vegetables and grains. Other people may choose to meet their requirements for food by eating a staple diet of meat and two vegetables. In some parts of our world even finding clean drinking water and food can be a major challenge. Human beings also have a need for connection, meaning and purpose. Life would seem very bleak if we did not have the opportunity to love and be loved, or to find meaning in our daily interactions and activities.

Our needs are closely connected to our thinking, feeling and behaviors. If our physical needs such as eating regularly or sleeping well are not met then this can lead to irritability because your ability to cope with life may be impaired. Equally if your needs for shelter and security are not met because you find yourself moving from one temporary home to another then this can lead to depression and other physical symptoms such as poor digestion and low energy. Becoming dehydrated through not drinking enough clean water can also impair the ability to concentrate. In recent years, for example, schools, colleges and workplaces have installed water coolers because having the opportunity to drink more water, on a daily basis, is a way of improving concentration levels.

After your basic survival needs for air, food, clean water and shelter have been met, you will develop other preferences, which are important to your overall well-being. These preferences may seem like needs yet upon closer inspection we will see the difference between them. For example, if we need to be in control this can limit our lives because it can prevent flexible thinking. The need for control may also be connected to wanting to be right which is likely to generate conflict when communicating with others. In contrast, if we prefer to be in control but can also act flexibly, this will be more beneficial to our interaction with others.

Fergus's Story

Fergus had an excessive need to be busy and important. These two needs were closely connected. Fergus went around telling his friends, family and co-workers how busy he was. He also felt important because he had an overflowing in-tray and large 'to do' list. Fergus rarely left work behind, he used his laptop and mobile telephone while travelling and even on holiday. It was the onset of a serious heart condition that changed things for Fergus. After a stint in hospital he realized that work was taking over his life and impacting upon his physical and mental well-being. A few months later Fergus took early retirement from his employer and is far happier. After retiring Fergus took up an interest in researching family history and also got involved in local committee work. Once his fast-paced work habits were over, he also looked much younger and felt healthier.

The following list may help you identify some of your needs:

To be accepted	To be accomplished	To be adored
To be cared for	To be right	To be indulged
To be in control	To be in command	To be useful
To be calm	To be peaceful	To be informed
To be listened to	To please others	To be devoted to a cause

Exercise

From this list start to identify which needs are life enhancing and which might be limiting for you. You could also list how these needs are impacting upon your life.

Attempting to manipulate the world around us so that we can satisfy our needs can be both futile and exhausting. One of the key principles of the law of attraction is that like attracts like. Some needs are more life enhancing than others. On some occasions the need to be commanding can be supportive, particularly if you are facing a particular dilemma and want to feel empowered. On other occasions being commanding might not be the most appropriate response when you are dealing with a particularly sensitive issue that requires a gentler approach. The following examples illustrate how our needs can be life enhancing, rather than restricting:

- We could choose to be peaceful to attract more peace into our lives;
- Instead of needing acceptance from the people around us, we could be more accepting;
- Rather than having a need to be cared for, we can be more caring;
- We can start to adore others rather than seeking to be adored.

Simon's Story

During coaching Simon realized that he had an excessive need to feel included and appreciated at work. Simon had worked for a large public sector organization, where he was part of a small close-knit team. The team had met regularly to discuss what they were doing and plan for the future. Simon's manager had also made a point of including all team members in discussions and they were also given the opportunity to contribute towards decision making. In addition the team had often met up during their leisure time and enjoyed activities such as hiking and bowling. Simon came to coaching because he had recently moved to a new organization. Although he was pleased to move to a new workplace because it resulted in a promotion, he did not feel included in his new team. Simon's new line manager was distant and seemed preoccupied with their problems. Simon's co-workers tended to group together at break times and he overheard them laughing about what they had done at weekends. Simon felt left out and started to question whether his new colleagues liked him, which made him even more anxious. As a result of his anxiety Simon was generating a sense of neediness which resulted in his new colleagues backing away from him. What was happening was that Simon was demanding to be accepted. He soon realized that this demand for inclusion was attracting unhelpful feelings of rejection and isolation. He also began to accept that feeling left out is a common experience when starting a new job. Simon realized that it was because he was regarded as the new guy, rather than some perceived personality faults that were leading to his feelings of being left out. Fortunately Simon was able to change things. Firstly he began to lighten up and not be overly concerned by the actions of his colleagues. When his neediness was reduced he found that his colleagues did start to approach him and ask him how he was getting on with his new role. A few weeks later there was an employee away day involving team-building exercises. Through joining group activities Simon soon began to feel included and make new friends.

As Simon's story indicates, when needs become unbalanced they can become demands. Simon discovered that demanding to be accepted by his new work colleagues did not attract positive relationships in the workplace. After Simon changed how he thought about his experiences with work colleagues and the workplace things started to shift in a more positive direction. Taking another example, think about what could happen if you demand to be right – what sorts of experiences will this tend to attract? How will you deal with disagreements and different points of view? Preferences, however, are less emotionally charged than needs and demands. If you prefer to be right, rather than demand to be right, this will probably foster helpful discussions with other people. For example, they might appreciate your willingness to be open to different points of view.

Imagine that you are looking forward to a quiet weekend away with a friend because you need some peace but find that you are staying in a hotel which is hosting a noisy wedding party. It is possible that you may become irritable because your sense of peace has been disturbed. In this situation flexible thinking can be incredibly useful. Firstly, the wedding party is not going to last forever. Furthermore there are several steps you could take to find some peace during your weekend away. Perhaps you could go prepared and take some earplugs, or use your portable music player to play soothing music through headphones to mask the sound of the party. You might also wake up early the next morning to find that a sense of peace permeates the hotel as the wedding party is recovering from their revelry the night before.

Often we think that putting the needs of others before our own is admirable but even this can be taken to extremes. Feeling that you need to please others to be accepted or popular can lead to resentment and loss of self-worth. We could even exhaust ourselves attempting to please others. Nonetheless, despite our best efforts, there is no guarantee that we can please others because they also have choices about how to respond to us. How might a need for appreciation, for example, impact upon your relationships with your partner? They could have different needs such as being powerful and in control. So perhaps they do not realize that you would like some appreciation for the things you do for them. Maybe you are someone who thrives on adventure but your partner needs to feel safe and secure. Talking with others about your needs is the first step in creating a sense of balance and improving the relationship.

Expecting friends and family members to satisfy your needs may not be helpful and may lead to conflict. Family members and friends could have their own challenges to deal with, or are preoccupied with other aspects of their life and may be unable to satisfy your needs. So you could explore the ways in which you can satisfy your own needs in a positive way. If you have a need for comfort, for instance, you may find it comforting to relax watching a heart-warming film, have a long soak in the bath, or for a special treat indulge in a slice of chocolate cake. Alternatively a need to be creative can be satisfied in many different ways, from taking up a hobby, attending a night class in a creative subject, or experimenting with cooking different dishes.

Beth's Story

Beth came to coaching because she was unhappy in her role as an administrator in a large public sector organization. Beth's parents were glad that she had settled down into what they considered a steady job with good prospects. Yet Beth longed to do something more creative. During her first coaching session Beth revealed that she wanted to develop her creative writing skills. Beth's current role involved providing administration services for committees which emphasized rules and regulations and required a methodical approach. Beth found that since her strength was creativity she felt stifled by her current role. She identified that being creative and self-directed were important aspects of her life. As Beth was in her mid-twenties she felt that she had plenty of time to explore other career options. It was apparent that Beth's creative impulses were not met in her current role and that it was time to make changes in this area of her life. Beth was already earning a small income from freelance writing alongside her current role. During coaching she explored the possibility of building upon her existing success. Seeing that it was possible to develop a career as a writer Beth's energy levels soared because she felt motivated and inspired. Within a year Beth had taken a voluntary redundancy package and used this as a springboard for her career change into a freelance writer.

It is important to discover, clarify and also find positive and enhancing ways to fulfill your preferences. The following exercise will help you do this.

Exercise

What are your top 5 needs?

How do you respond to unmet needs?

Have any of your needs become more like demands?

What are you currently doing to meet your needs?

Is what you are currently doing supporting your overall well-being?

If not, what are other ways of meeting your needs?

What are the advantages of having preferences rather than needs?

This chapter has highlighted the ways in which we have basic survival needs such as air, food, shelter and clean water but we also need love, connection and a sense of meaning and purpose in our lives. We have discovered that our unmet needs could have a detrimental impact upon our thinking, feeling and behavior because excessive needs become more like demands. Yet this often pushes away the experiences and things we are attempting to achieve. Remind yourself of the law of attraction, which is that likes attract like. So being loving is a way of attracting more love into our lives, rather than demanding it from others. Also attempting to satisfy the needs of others rather than your own needs can appear to be admirable but this can also become unbalanced if you are using it as a crutch so that you feel loved, appreciated, included or important. So find positive ways to fulfill your own needs rather than expecting other people to meet them.

Chapter Six

Taking Stock

You may be dissatisfied with your life at present and are ready to change but you do not know where to start. In this chapter you will learn the tools and techniques that will enable you to pinpoint what is functioning successfully in your life. You will also identify the particular areas you want to improve and see how the different parts of your life are connected.

Wheel of Life

What follows is a step-by-step guide to the wheel of life which is a well-known tool in life coaching that many coaching clients have found effective. The metaphor of the wheel is fitting because our lives keep on moving and there are connections between different parts of our lives just like the spokes of a wheel. For instance, our health can impact upon our relationships, or career. It may even stop us having fun and enjoying life to the full. Usually the wheel of life has eight segments based on different aspects of our lives such as career, family, relationships, finance, health, fitness and so forth. These segments are not set in stone, so you may choose to label them in different ways.

Start with a blank sheet of paper.

1. Write your name and the date on the paper so you have a record of when you completed this exercise. Dating your wheel of life will also allow you to track change, over time. Some people, for example, like to repeat this exercise on a monthly, quarterly or half-yearly basis.

2. Draw a circle and divide it into segments. You might want to use different colors for each of the segments.

3. Label each segment e.g. health, finance, career, fitness, close personal relationships, family, spirituality and fun. You can also use your own labels depending on what aspects of life you want to change.

4. Give each segment a rating out of 10 based on your current situation. For example, if you are feeling sluggish and unhealthy after developing a habit of snacking on junk food you might want to rate your health as 6 out of 10.

Now examine the results:

- Which areas of your life have a low score?
- Which areas of your life have a high score?
- How might these areas be connected?
- What areas of your life do you want to improve?
- Write down the positive and negative aspects of your current situation.
- Reflect upon the sorts of experiences you are attracting through your scores in each area.

5. Rate those areas you want to improve out of 10. For example, if you want to improve your career, from 4 out of 10 how high do you want this to be, 8, 9 or even 10?

6. Write down positive aspects and challenges you might face when changing the areas you have identified.

It is not necessary to aim at having a score of 10 in each area because this is impractical and can actually be de-motivating. At present there may be some temporary imbalance in your life, rather than an ongoing chronic sense of dissatisfaction. For example, you might be feeling unhealthy or sluggish after the Christmas season because you have eaten a lot of rich food and had little exercise. Nonetheless once you get back into your usual routine of eating well and exercising then your health will improve. The wheel of life can, however, be used to help you establish if you are engaging in longer-term habits that are not supportive such as overeating, excessive drinking, overworking or avoiding personal relationships. Remind yourself of the pay-offs for those areas which appear to be low rated. For example, lack of exercise and eating an imbalanced diet of too much junk food might be something that you find pleasurable. What is less enjoyable is the impact these habits are having upon your overall well-being.

Writing down the positive aspects of your current situation allows you to acknowledge those things that you do feel good about. You may score 8 or 9 in your career because you have just obtained a promotion after a solid track record of good performance. You might rate your close relationships highly due to the joy and fulfillment that they bring to your life. Maybe you have a regular fitness regime which is improving your fitness and increasing your energy levels.

The wheel of life exercise also enables you to consider the sorts of experiences that you are attracting. It may be that you score highly in the area of spirituality and this attracts experiences and situations that allow you to express this aspect of your life. For example, due to your spiritual beliefs you may cherish animals and choose to volunteer at an animal sanctuary, or buy products which are not harmful to animals. Conversely, if you have a low score for friendship because you find it difficult to trust others then this may draw isolation and feelings of loneliness into your life.

When you have identified the areas you want to change, think about how these changes will impact upon others. For example, how might the changes you want to make impact upon your relationships with your partner, family members, work colleagues and friends? If you want to switch careers how might this impact upon your finances? Re-training for another career path could also impact upon time spent with your loved ones. Maybe you want to have a luxurious holiday as a reward for working hard but your partner needs a new car. Perhaps you can discuss your plans and work out ways to achieve them without impacting negatively upon others. Instead of having a luxurious holiday, you could decide to have a short weekend break. You could opt for a stand-by holiday deal, which can often be considerably cheaper than booking in advance. Your partner may decide that it would be acceptable to buy a cheaper, second-hand car so that you can still have a holiday, even if it is not as luxurious as originally planned.

Attempting to change all areas of your life at the same time can be overwhelming. Imagine moving house, changing job, starting a new part-time training course and planning to run a marathon all at the same time – this would be exhausting. After completing your scores in different parts of your life, move on to make decisions about which areas you want to change first. Some people highlight just one area they want to focus on, whereas others choose three or four. Reflect upon what works for you and which areas are most important to you at the present time.

Finally this exercise involves mapping out the positive changes you want to bring into different parts of your life and starting to think of some of the challenges you might face along the way. For example, if you decide to improve your financial situation it can be very motivating to think about the positive changes this will bring. How will you feel when you are debt free? What will it be like to see your investments grow? On the other hand, what challenges might you face to improving your financial situation, such as an unexpected bill, or a major item of expenditure?

The wheel of life exercise works just as well in the form of a list, or chart. Here is an example of a completed list which demonstrates how you can adapt this exercise:

Name: Jamie Green
Date: 5th January 2011

Area of life	Current rating	Desired rating
Career	4	7
Relationship with partner	6	7
Family	8	8
Finance	5	7
Friends	8	8
Fun	8	8
Health and fitness	2	6
Personal development	2	6
Spirituality	6	6

Jamie is in his late twenties and has been married for a couple of years. Five years ago he started working as a customer adviser at a major insurance company. Jamie enjoys his job and has many friends within the company. Jamie's weakness is that he is a heavy drinker. Shortly after starting this job he began to relax by going out with his colleagues for drinks after work on Fridays. Now, he goes to bars to drink at lunchtimes as well. Jamie is also spending more time socializing and drinking than exercising or eating healthy food. As a result Jamie is focusing on drinking and having a good time rather than personal development or his career. His lunchtime visits to bars is also becoming an expensive habit which is impacting upon his finances. Jamie is not an alcoholic; but he is a social drinker. He uses drinking as a way of bonding with friends and unwinding after work. After completing this exercise, Jamie started to realize that his social drinking habits were impacting negatively on other parts of his life.

Jamie's lowest rated areas:

Health and fitness	2
Personal development	2
Career	4
Finance	5

After reflecting upon his current ratings for different aspects of his life, Jamie identified which areas he wanted to change and what would bring him a sense of satisfaction in these areas. For example, Jamie wanted to initially increase his health and fitness from a rating of 2 to 6. Jamie thought that this level of increase would be motivating, rather than attempting to reach a level 8 or 9 straight away. However, Jamie felt that it was time to give more focus to his career and move this from a level 4 to 7.

Jamie also produced a written list of the positive and negative aspects of his current situation.

Positive aspects:
- Enjoying friendships;
- Relaxing;
- Working for a well-regarded employer;
- Steady wage;
- Having a supportive relationship.

Negative aspects:
- Being careless and inattentive at work;
- Wasting time;
- Unhealthy eating and drinking habits;
- Feeling unfit;
- Letting career opportunities pass by;
- Not making the most of career options with current employer;
- Wasting money.

Upon reflection Jamie realized that his current life situation was attracting the following thoughts, feelings and behaviors:

Thoughts:
I'm wasting money on drinking.
Why didn't I sign up for that training course on project management last month?
How will I pay for my car insurance next month?

Feelings:
Guilty   Bored   Apathetic

Behaviors:
Consuming too much alcohol;
Putting in the minimum effort at work;
Hiding bank statements in a drawer.

Going through each area of his life, Jamie was able to explore a number of options to increase his level of satisfaction and sense of fulfillment including:

- Establishing an after work football club on Fridays. After playing football Jamie intended to reward himself with two drinks and stick to this limit;
- Starting to bring packed lunches to work to avoid going to bars, thereby saving money;
- Finding out what training courses or workshops on self-development were available through his workplace;
- Investigating forthcoming conferences and seminars on self-development through his employer and also with other organizations or special interest groups;
- Asking about mentoring and secondment (reassignment) opportunities with current employer;

- Opening a savings account and making a commitment to set aside a small amount each month.

There were several positive aspects to the changes Jamie agreed to make including:

- An increasing sense of well-being after reducing alcohol intake;
- Learning new things and developing new skills through studying or attending workshops;
- Asking about mentoring or secondment opportunities at work;
- Having a sustainable savings plan in place which will gradually reap dividends.

Jamie also identified some of the challenges he could face whilst making positive changes in his life. These challenges included:

- Temptation to continue to drink alcohol;
- Peer pressure;
- Force of habit;
- Doubting own abilities;
- Balancing work and study time;
- Office politics and power games;
- Unexpected expenses.

After mapping out the areas he wanted to change, Jamie considered how these changes would impact upon his partner, family, work colleagues and friends. Firstly he thought that his friends might not be as supportive as he would like because they were stuck in their drinking habits. By changing his social drinking habits he would no longer be 'one of the lads'. On the other hand, Jamie thought that if he successfully reduced his alcohol intake then his friends might be inspired to do the same.

Additionally Jamie realized that developing new skills or taking a course of study would impact upon his relationship with his partner, time and finances. Seeking out mentoring and secondment opportunities at work would also require cultivating positive relationships with his manager and staff development department. Initially taking on a new role could be time consuming and may impact upon relationships with partner, family and friends. Jamie considered the sorts of thoughts, feelings and behaviors these positive changes will attract into his life:

Thoughts:
I can change my drinking habits.
I have the willpower and commitment to save regularly.
I am learning amazing new things.
I am developing my career with my current employer and also gaining valuable skills and experience which will make me more attractive to other employers.

Feelings:
Energetic   optimistic   interested   excited

Behavior:
Scheduling and completing studies;
Attending networking events, training courses and seminars;
Visiting the bank on a monthly basis to update savings account.

Jamie's example gives you some ideas about how you can use the wheel of life (or your list) to work through the changes you want to make in your life. For some people moving away from an undesirable state, such as feeling unhappy at work, or living in a cramped apartment, or constantly worrying about money is the starting point for change.

Kai's Story

Kai was a well-qualified human resources officer in local government. Unfortunately his manager John frequently undermined him. John was in his late fifties and had started working for the council after leaving school and had worked his way up in the organization. In contrast, Kai was in his early thirties and had attended university, obtaining both an undergraduate degree and postgraduate qualifications. Kai was ambitious so he wanted to undertake a professional qualification. He also wanted to have some flexibility regarding his working hours which would enable him to study effectively. John, however, stood in his way and insisted that there was very little flexibility in working hours due to the current workload and staffing levels in the department. Kai started to think, "I'll show John, he will not stand in my way." Over time, this thought of showing John that he would be successful, no matter what, was incredibly motivating for Kai. Indeed Kai would imagine coming into work after successfully completing his professional course and gloat while giving John a copy of his certificate. Kai's sense of bitterness and resentment towards John was slowly increasing. Although Kai was doing well on his course, he felt less committed to his job. These thoughts and feelings meant that he was putting in a great deal of effort in his study assignments but was becoming sloppy at work. He also started to feel guilty about his fantasies of gloating when completing his course. These feelings of guilt, bitterness and resentment were attracting unsupportive behaviors in the workplace and lead to dissatisfaction with his job, department and employer. In the end, after successfully completing his professional course, Kai looked for another job and in a few months had moved to another organization.

So for some people moving away from something will initially be motivating, yet it is important to remember that this could be underpinned by thoughts, feelings and behaviors that over the long-term are not affirming and will not attract good experiences. It is quite common to focus on what we do not want, rather than what we do want to change. As Bill McFarlan points out in his book *Drop the Pink Elephant,* focusing on what you do not want attracts the thoughts, feelings and behaviors that you are attempting to avoid. For example, if you are constantly thinking about not wanting to be poor, you may start to focus on things like unpaid bills, mounting debt or paying for birthday presents or expensive Christmas gifts. You could also start to feel depressed about the things you believe that you cannot have due to lack of money such as a holiday, home renovation, new clothes or eating out. These thoughts and feelings can lead to behaviors such as holding on to money too tightly, in other words being stingy. After a while these thoughts, feelings and behaviors could start a backlash. You may start to feel fed up with not spending and want to treat yourself so you go to a shopping center and have a splurge on a new outfit. You are initially thrilled by your new purchases but this evaporates once your credit card bill arrives. The following examples demonstrate how using 'I don't want' focuses on the very thing you are attempting to avoid:

Statement	Focuses on
I don't want to be poor	**poverty**
I don't want to be overweight	**weight**
I don't want to work for a big company	**working for a big company**
I don't want to get married	**getting married**
I don't want to get stuck in traffic	**getting stuck in traffic**
I don't want to smoke	**smoking**
I don't want to do any more studying	**studying**

| I don't want to join a gym | **joining a gym** |
| I don't want to go out tonight | **going out** |

Concentrating on what you do want will attract the thoughts, feelings and behaviors that are more likely to draw these things to you. Here are some examples of how to change unhelpful statements into something more positive:

- I don't want to be poor becomes **I want to feel a sense of abundance**
- I don't want to overweight becomes **I want to develop healthy eating habits**
- I don't want to work for a large organization becomes **I want to work for small company**
- I don't want to be married becomes **I want to have a relationship that suits me and my partner**
- I don't want to get stuck in rush hour traffic becomes **I want to arrive at work in good time**
- I don't want to smoke becomes **I want to be smoke free**
- I don't want to study becomes **I want to find out what sorts of learning opportunities would best suit my needs**
- I don't want to join a gym becomes **I want to find out what sorts of exercise will work best for me**
- I don't want to go out tonight becomes **I want to relax by staying in**

Now the focus is on:

- Wealth
- Health
- Working for a small organization
- A fulfilling relationship
- Arriving at work in good time
- Being smoke free

- Learning opportunities that suit your needs
- A form of exercise that suits you
- Staying at home relaxing

Exercise:

Think about your own experiences; are you focusing on what you don't want instead of what you do want?

Write down examples of when you focus on what you do not want.

Rewrite your examples in positive language so they focus to what you do want.

During this chapter you have clarified what areas of life you want to change and how to formulate positive statements about what you want. You can now consider the interactions between different parts of your life. What are the positive and negative aspects of your current situation – what is going well and what could be better? Identify three or four areas you want to change, rather than attempting to change everything all at once. Also consider the positive and negative aspects of your proposed changes. The most important thing is to focus on what you do want, rather than what you do not want. In the next chapter we will move on to consider the values and beliefs that are important to you and how they relate to your life experiences.

Chapter Seven

Values and Beliefs

In this chapter you will consider how your values and beliefs relate to your thoughts, feelings and behaviors. Values are those things that you hold dear, they give meaning to your life. Your values and beliefs may be influenced by various sources such as education, religion and the media. Sometimes you can take on socially acceptable values and beliefs. Yet there may be a feeling of uncertainty as other, more authentic values start to emerge within you. You may be drawn to those people who have similar values and beliefs to your own because they seem to be on the same wavelength. On the other hand, you could find it difficult to relate to someone who has very different beliefs, especially if they seem to violate the things you value. You will probably be able to identify when your values are not met because this often generates discomfort within you. Even so, it is important to attempt to understand the values and beliefs of others rather than simply reject them.

In this chapter you will investigate values and beliefs and identify those which are working well for you, bringing you life affirming experiences and those which are not. Here we will also be dealing with issues such as your level of self-belief. By doing so you will start to understand how your values and beliefs relate to your life experiences. During the exercises in this chapter you will have the opportunity to identify those situations when your values or beliefs were not met. You will then consider how the changes you want to make in your life are motivated by your values and beliefs. It is possible that your values or beliefs change over time as you encounter new experiences and learn about new things. During this chapter you may also discover that you have beliefs about beliefs!

Values

Values are what you find meaningful and important in your life; they give your life clarity and direction. It is important to clarify your values before you start to set goals to bring changes into your life. If you ignore this stage of your journey towards change, then you may set goals that are not aligned to what you value the most. So, even if you do achieve your goal you may not feel satisfied.

Punctuality

One of my strong values is punctuality. As a result I tend to plan ahead for meetings, visiting friends and travelling to conferences and workshops. When attending an event in a nearby town, I visited the location beforehand and obtained travel information to ensure that I was thoroughly prepared. I arrived at fifteen minutes before the event started and used this time to get settled into my new surroundings. Because I value punctuality I have a tendency to get annoyed when I have arranged to meet friends and they show up late. When my friends do not turn up on time I have sometimes thought this is disrespectful and shows a lack of commitment to our friendship. After investigating my values I realized that I was becoming a stickler for punctuality. Furthermore, when friends showed up late I was starting to engage in negative thoughts, feelings and behaviors.

Here are some of the ways in which the value of punctuality was impacting upon my experiences:

Thoughts:

My friend must arrive on time.

They don't care about me; if they did they would make an effort to be here on time.

I am just wasting time waiting around.

There are other, more enjoyable things I could be doing than waiting here.

Feelings:

Anxiety

Frustration

Behavior:

Looking at my watch every few minutes

Pacing up and down

Checking my mobile phone for messages.

Because I was focusing on the undesirable aspects of punctuality this is what was showing up in my life in the form of friends being late on a regular basis or the cancellation of appointments. In one week, I noted that 4 out of 5 of my meetings were cancelled. In addition I found myself waiting around for a friend for half an hour until they finally showed up.

I knew that my value of punctuality was becoming too extreme and started to explore other ways of thinking. To begin with, I began to realize that my friends may not know how important this value is to me. When my friends were late, they tended to apologize profusely. I would often just let it go by saying that it didn't matter that they were late. Yet underneath this façade of acceptance I was sometimes feeling annoyed. I realized that it was possible to be more assertive about the value of punctuality and explain to friends that this was important to me. The next time my friend showed up late, I calmly and firmly stated that I had noticed that this was a regular occurrence and that it bothered me. My friend admitted that she had no idea how important punctuality was to me and would make an extra effort to be punctual next time we met.

I also decided to lighten up a little with regards to punctuality; it is still an important issue for me but it isn't the end of the world when a friend is late. I also made a point of changing my thoughts, feelings and behaviors to ones that were more supportive:

Thoughts:
I look forward to meeting my friend and if they are late it is not a major disaster.

I understand that it is not always possible to be on time due to traffic, work commitments or some unexpected event.

If my friend is late again I will be more assertive and point out that I feel annoyed waiting around for them.

Feelings:
Patience
Understanding

Behavior:
Enjoying surroundings while waiting for friends. I particularly like to people watch. On one occasion while waiting for a friend I enjoyed listening to a street musician who was playing some amazing jazz tunes.

When I started being more assertive with friends who were consistently late this cleared the air and removed my frustration. After making these changes, I have found a greater sense of honesty by expressing my values. I have also found that by lightening up my attitude to punctuality I am less tense and anxious about any delays. I also started to notice that I am no longer attracting the same levels of cancellation of meetings or events into my life.

Below are some other examples that illustrate how our values relate to our lives.

- Your partner buys you a surprise gift.
  (values – appreciation, love)

- You have a few items to take to the supermarket checkout and the person in front has a huge trolley (basket) of food and they let you go ahead of them.
  (values – kindness, consideration of others)

- You have a group of friends round for a party and enjoy talking until the early hours of the morning.
  (values – friendship, connection, communication)

- You have just finished a watercolor painting and feel a wonderful sense of accomplishment through expressing your creativity.
  (values – creativity, fun)

- For the past few months you have worked extra hours and learned new skills to complete an important project. As a result you feel a sense of achievement and contribution to your workplace.
  (values – contribution, accomplishment)

- You have just started a new course and are excited by learning new things thereby contributing to your self-development.
  (values – knowledge, self-development)

It is worthwhile reflecting on what you value since this will influence various aspects of your life. The things that you value will motivate you because they are meaningful and important. Once you clarify your values it is easier to formulate an action plan with goals that are aligned with your values and support your view of life. As a result, when you do meet your goals you will feel a greater sense of accomplishment.

Reflecting on your recent experiences, think about what sorts of experiences honor your values? When have your values been challenged? You may want to write your answers in a journal so that you can map your thoughts and create a body of evidence that clarifies and supports your values.

Below are some examples of values:

Humor	Integrity	Accomplishment
Focus	Freedom	Excellence
Honesty	Creativity	Loyalty
Performance	Perfection	Self-expression
Nurturing	Partnership	Zest for life
Joy	Independence	Authenticity
Growth	Adventure	Contribution
Service	Power	Participation
Success	Connection	Harmony
Risk	Romance	Peace
Sharing	Trust	Vitality
Commitment	Dedication	Appreciation

Ajay's Story

Ajay was a young executive who came to coaching in order to improve his work life balance. Ajay had two small children, one at nursery, the other at primary school. Ajay's partner also had a demanding full-time job. After completing an exercise on values, Ajay realized that what mattered to him was commitment, partnership, connection and harmony. Family life was extremely important to Ajay but his present work situation was of working long hours both during the week and at weekends. Ajay often returned home at 8pm when the children had gone to bed and only saw them for a few minutes each morning before he set off for work. Even when he spent time with his family, Ajay was thinking about work and worrying about all the things he needed to do when he went back to the office. Ajay felt that he was missing out on valuable time with his partner and children. During the coaching process Ajay decided to explore ways of finding greater balance in life and concentrating on those things he valued. As a result Ajay approached his employer and reduced his hours from 38 to 32 per week, over four days. While this meant a drop in salary, this was offset by having more time with his family. Working four days instead of five also saved on commuting to and from work. Ajay also found other ways to reduce his workload. He acknowledged that he was not good at trusting others with projects and made an effort to change this. Ajay trained a junior member of staff, who was eager to take on new project work and this alleviated some of his former workload.

You may be in similar position to Ajay, living in a way that does not support your values. If so, this may be manifesting in your life as feeling pressured, unwell, out of kilter or just a general sense of background dissatisfaction. The following exercise takes you step-by-step into understanding and clarifying your values, so that you can start to make changes in your life based on what is most important to you.

Exercise
Choose your current top 10 values and write them down.
Rank your values in importance, 1=most important, 10=least
  important.
*You can also create your own values, if they do not appear on
  this list.
Reflect upon how difficult or easy it was to rank these values.
Do your values form particular clusters of meaning (for
  example, peace and harmony, or independence and

adventure)?

What sort of experiences are your values attracting into your life?

Assessing Roles and Values

You may be playing many different roles in your life. These roles may also change over time. You might be a community worker for a couple of years and this might develop into the role of a councilor or politician. In other cases, your role as an employee might change if you are made redundant, retire or become self-employed. You may also take on mythical roles and identify with them. For example, you may consider yourself the rescuer, the saint or the clown. A mythical role such as the adventurer can be empowering but the role of the rescuer, as detailed in the story below, may be less helpful.

Sally's Story

Sally took on the role of the rescuer and attracted experiences that helped her fulfill this role. She seemed to attract friends who needed help such as car rides, small amounts of money, or child-minding. At first Sally enjoyed this role because it made her feel wanted and useful. She got a buzz from helping other people. Offering to help friends is a positive thing but what happened to Sally was that over time she received so many requests for help that she started to feel overwhelmed. One week she noticed that she had received the following requests:

- A friend called to ask for a car ride to work because she was running late;
- A neighbor asked her to feed her cat while she was away for a couple of days;
- Her sister asked her if she could look after her two children one evening;

- Her son and daughter-in-law asked if they could have some money to help pay an unexpected bill;
- A co-worker was stressed due to completing a large project and asked if would Sally help out;
- An elderly acquaintance went into hospital and since their family lived some distance away they asked Sally if she could visit him and report back to them.

Sally was juggling so many things that she started to feel under pressure. Instead of feeling wanted and helpful, she began to feel used. Her friends, neighbors, family and co-workers had become so accustomed to Sally helping them out that they continued to make demands on her. She was like a one-stop-social service. When Sally became ill she was unable to fulfill the role of rescuer for other people. What happened was that her friends, family, co-workers and neighbors had either found other people to help them out or had coped themselves. Consequently Sally came to the realization that she did not need to play the role of the rescuer.

Stepping back from your roles can help you see if it is supporting your best interests. It may also be a question of balance since used in moderation a particular mythical role might be beneficial. At times we may need to take on the role of adventurer, to step out of our comfort zone and do new things. If the occasion calls for it, the role of the clown may be appropriate; yet at other times it can be limiting. For example if we take on the role of clown at the office Christmas party we may entertain our co-workers but if we continue this role in the office this may limit our promotion prospects because we are not taken seriously.

When you take on different roles you may behave and communicate in different ways. For example, you might talk differently when answering a business phone call, to answering a message from your friend on a mobile telephone. These roles also involve drawing upon different values. Your working life might be based around values such as power or teamwork, whereas your close relationships might be founded upon values such as trust, honesty and fun.

The list below indicates some of the roles you might take on during your life:

Mother-Father	Daughter-Son	Grandparent
Husband-Wife	Grandchild	Aunt-Uncle
Nephew-Niece	Cousin	Friend
Manager	Supervisor	Colleague
Volunteer	Councilor	Politician
Community worker	Activist	Band member
Learner	The fool	Teacher
Neighbor	Lover	Writer
Planner	Organizer	Facilitator
Leader	Visionary	Entertainer

You might also interpret your roles in a variety of ways. For example, you might have a job that you really enjoy because it allows you to take on roles such as facilitator, or organizer. A key role that is often overlooked is the role of friend to yourself. You might be a loyal, trustworthy and supportive friend to others, yet highly critical of yourself. If you do not honor your values in the different roles in your life then this can create tension and imbalance. Perhaps deep down you know that you are not honoring what is really important to you.

Sandeep's Story
Sandeep was a member of a busy sales team who found the roles and values exercise particularly useful. In particular he found that while he valued harmony, peace and honesty the work place culture seemed to value competition over and above anything else. Sandeep explained that a chart was displayed in the office each week that gave sales figures for

each member of the team. The company also gave a bonus to the best-selling member of the team. For some people this environment would have been a way to motivate them to be competitive. For Sandeep, though, this work environment generated conflict between his values and the ways in which he perceived that his sales were pitted against his co-workers. Over time Sandeep began to detest the values of his workplace but through coaching he was able to formulate an action plan to retrain and switch career track. After retraining Sandeep is now a self-employed nutritionist who is able to exercise his values of peace, honesty and harmony to help others create and maintain healthy eating habits. Furthermore, the marketing and selling skills that he used in his previous job were tremendously helpful when he came to starting his own business.

Exercise

The following exercise involves questioning how you are demonstrating your values through the different roles in your life.

1. Who are the most important people in my life?
2. How am I demonstrating those values, which are important to me through my role as .... (complete the blank with your chosen role)?
3. What would your day be like if you focused on what you value the most?

Beliefs

Beliefs are a collection of thoughts that you hold to be true. You will probably base the truth of your beliefs on evidence from a variety of sources including your own experiences, other people, books, journals, magazines, newspaper articles, experts or television programs. Facts are often neutral and informative, whereas beliefs can be highly emotionally charged. The factual information about your employment, for example, includes the name of your employer, the address of the office, the number of years you have worked for the company, your job title and salary. As well as these factual aspects of your employment, you may have emotional feelings that are associated with beliefs about your employment. You may have beliefs about the integrity of the company, or you may believe that the number of years in employment entitles you to a promotion. You could also believe that work is an opportunity to share your unique talents. On the other hand you could believe that work is a form of drudgery.

There are different levels of beliefs; some of our beliefs might be easily swayed while others are deeply ingrained. Some beliefs are so ingrained that they become a fundamental part of our identity. You may believe that you are too old to change, to learn a new skill or change careers. In this case, the belief that you are too old is a limitation because it is preventing you from exploring the changes that could bring new experiences into your life.

Maggie's Story

Maggie certainly did not believe that she was too old for anything. After raising three children, she decided to study leisure and tourism at college. She successfully completed her college course and in her mid-fifties went on to university and obtained a degree. Maggie then started to formulate plans to emigrate to Australia to be closer to her son. Five years later when her finances and documentation were approved Maggie moved to Australia. By Maggie's sixty-fifth birthday she found herself in a new country, had obtained a part-time job, passed her driving test and bought a new house. She obtained a second-hand car and enjoyed exploring new places. Maggie certainly did not believe that she was too old to change and at an age when most people are thinking about retirement and winding down she was creating a whole new chapter of her life.

You may not realize that your beliefs have an impact upon your thoughts, emotional states and behaviors. By identifying your beliefs it is possible to evaluate them to see if they are helpful or not. If your beliefs are not supportive, you can begin to change them. Often deep-seated beliefs develop in childhood and you may have retained them, even when they no longer support you. Your beliefs may also have developed through relationships with friends, family, colleagues and teachers. Beliefs can also be formed in response to what you read about in the newspaper, see on television or at the cinema. You might also take on beliefs through your religion (or spiritual/personal philosophy), political affiliations, the workplace, or membership of certain groups. Each person has their own unique collection of beliefs due to their life history and experiences. While a person has a particular collection of beliefs that is unique, the beliefs themselves are meaningful in a social and cultural context. The actions that can arise from holding some beliefs can, for example, be regarded as unacceptable or illegal if they result in the physical or mental harm of others. So while it is important to attempt to gain some understanding why a person holds a certain belief it is also necessary to question the outcome of that belief, in a wider context. Even the most personal beliefs we have about our mental or physical capabilities or appearance can impact upon those around us.

For example, you might believe that it is necessary to be academically brilliant to be successful in life. You may have picked up this belief from a variety of sources:

- Your parents/guardians might say that you will never get a good job if you don't study really hard;
- Your teachers may issue warnings about what will happen if you fail your exams;
- Your friends are high achievers and aspire to go to university and you will feel left out if you do not go to university;

- You may read newspaper reports about the lack of job prospects for those without a degree.

However, it is important to question the validity of such beliefs. What evidence is there that you need to be academically brilliant to be successful in life? What evidence counters this belief? Does being successful mean different things to different people? For example, a person with a degree or a highly-paid professional their career might feel empty or unfilled – so are they successful or not? Think of people who are successful (even famous people) who have triumphed in their field without having achieved academic success at a young age. Lord Alan Sugar, for instance, left school with few qualifications yet he has become an incredibly successful entrepreneur.

In some cases it can be challenging to abandon your beliefs as you grow and change through life experience. You may have become so used to your beliefs that you are not sure what to do when they are no longer supporting you. For example, you may have the belief that money is in short supply or that there is never enough to make ends meet. This might have been a valid belief when you were just starting out as a junior employee, living on limited finances. However, you may still hold on to this belief even when you have gained several promotions, increased your salary and received additional company benefits. By holding on to this belief about not having enough money, you could drive yourself to work harder and put extra pressure on yourself just to keep on earning more and more.

Some of your beliefs could be very powerful while others are more like attitudes or assumptions. So while you may be persuaded to discard some beliefs others are extremely entrenched. Judith Beck, a successful and renowned cognitive therapist, has identified three main levels of beliefs. At the first level are automatic thoughts that are based on our beliefs and have become habitual through repetition. Secondly there are intermediate beliefs such as attitudes and assumptions. Then there are core beliefs, deeply ingrained thoughts about ourselves, others and the world around us. Beliefs are often so habitual that we fail to question them and simply take them for granted. But by questioning your beliefs you are opening up the possibility of finding new evidence that might shed a different light on them.

Jenny's Story

Following many enjoyable holidays in Spain, Jenny decided that she wanted to learn to speak Spanish. She enrolled for a course at a local college full of enthusiasm. After the first few lessons Jenny's negative beliefs surfaced and she started to feel that her studies were extremely difficult. These negative beliefs included thoughts such as it is better to learn a new language when you are young and that she would never pick up the language; she was finding it just too difficult. Jenny was also a perfectionist and mentally punished herself for getting a few phrases mixed up or not pronouncing them correctly. Jenny started to realize that her beliefs were not supporting her and began to explore other ways of thinking which would be more helpful. She turned things around by thinking that it is fine to be a learner and not know all the answers; it may take time to develop her language skills. She also started to notice the things that were improving in her studies rather than the few mistakes she made. Jenny reinforced these alternative beliefs by finding evidence to support them.

For example, Jenny noted the following:

- She found that her confidence regarding language skills increased by practicing with a family member;
- She spoke in Spanish for half an hour and only made a couple of mistakes;

- She started learning how to correct mistakes through feedback from her tutor;
- She received a good marks for her first assignment;
- She started to investigate and find examples of other mature students who have been successful.

There is a common saying that seeing is believing; in other words if you see something then you will believe it. However, in *You'll See it When You Believe It*, Wayne Dyer turns this around by showing that when you believe something then you will see it. When you believe something to be true you are likely to find evidence to support it and discard any evidence that challenges it. Since you may have an emotional attachment to your beliefs you take them as the truth and can become angry and defensive when they are challenged. Defensive thoughts, feelings and behaviors can then lead to conflict between thinking you are right and the other person is wrong. This prevents you from gaining an understanding of another person's point of view. The other person may have equally good reasons for believing what they do. You can ask the person to provide more information about what they believe, attempt to understand them even though you may not agree with them. Also we may find that we are drawn to people, events or experiences that reinforce our beliefs and values.

Jamil's Story
Jamil had just started business studies at a college in the North of England and started to have doubts about the quality and value of teaching he was receiving. As a result of these doubts, Jamil started to believe that the college was not a good academic institution.

Jamil then came up with several reasons that supported this belief including:

- The tutors did not explain things properly;
- Ten to fifteen minutes of lessons were spent filling in the register, handing out reading material and waiting for other students to arrive. So Jamil felt that he was getting about 45 minutes learning out of the one hour teaching slot;
- The office support staff did not pass on messages to the tutors;
- The office failed to ring Jamil to let him know when lessons were cancelled.

Furthermore, Jamil seemed to attract people and experiences that supported his belief. Returning home by train after the first term, Jamil started to chat to his fellow passenger, Steve. They started to talk about business studies and Steve asked Jamil which college he was studying at. Steve rolled his eyes when Jamil told him where he was studying. Steve retorted that he had a bad experience with this college because he had spent thousands of pounds on tuition but failed his exams. After switching courses and going to another college, Steve had made rapid progress and passed his exams. This conversation reinforced Jamil's beliefs about the quality and standards of the college he attended. Jamil began to become increasingly angry and frustrated with the college which impacted negatively upon his ability to learn. What happened was that Jamil became so concerned with his beliefs about quality and standards that he overlooked the things that might balance out his views such as:

- The times when the office did telephone to let him know of changes to his lessons;
- The tutors at the college were highly skilled and experienced and had completed lengthy training courses before taking on their roles;
- The college provided good support services to students

such as a 24/7 library service, a free e-mail account and
workshops on study skills;
- The college had received good quality and standard
reports   from external auditors;
- The college had a good track record for employability.

While Jamil began to recognize that his beliefs might be
impacting negatively upon his experience, it was still important
for him to consider the overall experience with his college before
deciding what to do next.

Beliefs impact on the different aspects of your life, the work
you do, your finances, relationships, self-development, or ability
to have fun. Here are some examples of how negative beliefs
operate in different parts of life

Work – is a chore, it pays the bills but it is not enjoyable

Money – corrupts, does not bring happiness and makes people
greedy

Self-development – is indulgent, expensive and time consuming

Relationships – are too demanding, or restricting

Fun – is something you do after you have worked hard, not
before

Health – it is too much time and effort to cook healthy from
scratch

Alternatively here are some positive beliefs about the same
aspects of life:

Work – is a way of serving others, of using my skills, knowledge
and abilities

Money – is meant to flow, to be shared

Self-development – is an investment

Relationships – are a way of growing and developing qualities
such as love, compassion, patience and understanding

Fun – and enjoyment are what makes life worthwhile

Health – the benefits of healthy home cooked nutritious food far outweighs the effort required to make it.

Changing your deep-rooted beliefs can take time and repeated practice. Here is an example of how to challenge negative beliefs and turn them around so that they are more positive.

Belief: beef burgers make you fat

- Do all beef burgers make you fat? What about low fat grilled rather than fried burgers?
- If burgers are an occasional treat and part of a balanced diet will eating them result in weight gain?
- Do burgers really make you fat – or is it your food choices and eating habits that lead to weight gain?

An even more powerful way to dispel beliefs is to provide evidence that they may not be true, or are not supporting you in creating a positive life. Here are a couple of examples that illustrate how this process works: A common belief is that there is never enough money. To counter this belief, make an inventory of all the items you possess. Go into detail, pretend you are stock taking. You will be astonished to find out how much stuff you actually have. In just one room of your house you may find: a kettle, 12 mugs, 6 cups and saucers, 4 bowls, 24 pieces of cutlery, a tin opener, bottle opener, 2 frying pans, a steamer, a rice cooker, toaster, microwave, washing machine, washing up liquid, household cleaning products, tins of soup, tea, coffee, sugar, fruit bowl, an iron, ironing board, table, 4 chairs etc... Writing down each item in this way is a powerful way of showing how much abundance there is in your life, even if you initially did not believe this. It may be that you have started to take these things for granted so this exercise can jolt you into a new sense of gratitude for what you do have.

Simply acquiring more and more material things does not necessarily bring us happiness. Often it is experiences and relationships that bring joy and fulfillment into our lives. You may find joy when watching a beautiful sunrise, walking in nature, talking to our loved ones, the picture that your son or daughter has painted for you at school, or playing with your dog or cat. By focusing on these joyful experiences you will start to overcome feelings of scarcity or not having enough. Instead you will appreciate the wonderful experiences that are already in your life. This will encourage you to find ways of drawing more joyful experiences to you.

Another common belief is that there is not enough time to do all the things you want to do. To counter this belief it is necessary to be completely honest and thorough about how you are using your time. You could start by writing down your daily activities for a two-week period. Reflect upon how much time you spending surfing the Internet, social networking, watching television, or sleeping. Also how much of your time at work is spent gossiping with colleagues, or dealing with interruptions? Often this exercise brings up resistance, such as thinking that watching television is a way to unwind after a hard day at work. However, is there a way you can reduce your television watching while still enjoying the occasional relaxing viewing experience? Even reducing your television watching or Internet surfing by 20 or 30 minutes per day will generate more time for other things. Another way of countering the belief of not having enough time is to start saying no to requests and invitations to meetings or events. A poorly considered acceptance is often worse than a well thought out refusal. For example do you really need to spend two hours in a meeting, or could you delegate that task? Could you read the minutes from the meeting when they are produced and then go to the next meeting when you do have more time?

You might have some resistance to changing your beliefs because you think they are part of your core personality. Because your beliefs often stem from your upbringing they can become a big part of our lives. As you get older you may become ruled by your beliefs and slip into a rut. This is why many old people find it difficult to change, such as to go out and make new friends. Sometimes when starting to change it is necessary to move towards something which seems believable for you, rather than simply adopting an opposing belief. For example, it might be quite a stretch to move from a belief that work is a chore to work is a means of service. Instead you may need to gradually shift your beliefs about work by investigating those things you do enjoy about working, or how your work impacts upon others. For example, you might start to notice that you get some enjoyment from organizing meetings and that this provides an important service to your company. Effective organization of meetings can, for example, result in maximizing time, or relationships with other departments or organizations.

Exercise

Write down your beliefs about work, money, relationships, health, self-development, or fun.

What evidence have you to support your beliefs?

What effect are your beliefs having on your life (e.g. career, personal relationships etc)?

Are your beliefs supporting your best interests?

How committed are you to changing this belief (on a scale of 1-10)?

What is the first step you can take to change your beliefs?

What can you do to reinforce your supportive beliefs?

What will you do long-term to maintain your positive beliefs?

We have now explored values that are those things you hold dear and are important to you. By identifying and clarifying which values are important, you can take steps to ensure that they are incorporated into your everyday life. You may now identify the different roles you may be playing in your personal and working life. You could be playing mythical roles, some of which are supportive such as the hero or the peacemaker, but others may be less supportive such as the role of the victim. Mapping the connection between your roles and values helps you identify where you are honoring what is important to you and other areas that you could improve. We have also discovered that beliefs are sets of ideas that stem from a number of sources, such as family background, religion, political affiliation, school and peers. Some beliefs are affirming but others could be limiting your experiences. By learning to question negative beliefs, you can start to turn them around and practice new ways of thinking. The next chapter delves more deeply into the use of words and phrases and the sorts of feelings and behaviors these can produce. You will be presented with examples of unconstructive language and may be able to identify some of these language practices in your own life. Several tools and techniques will be presented so that you can learn how to incorporate positive language into your daily life.

Chapter Eight

Words and Phrases

Words are symbols that are strung together in patterns or sequences which we find meaningful. The actual pattern of letters and words is not as important as the feelings or emotions that we associate with them. The pattern of letters that make up the word g-y-m might be associated with an enjoyable experience for one person but for other people this might conjure up feelings of strain and something they want to avoid. The feelings that are behind the words you use can be detected through tone of voice. Some people may say that they are feeling fine but use a flat tone of voice. In this case the tone of voice actually contradicts the words that are spoken.

People can also have different feelings or associations to the same word. In Yorkshire, for instance, there is a tradition of using the word *love* in all sorts of ways. When you enter a shop, or buy a bus ticket you might be asked, "What can I get you, love?" When you meet a neighbor on the street they may ask, "How are you, love?" For those who have not been brought up in Yorkshire, this use of the word *love* can seem very strange. Even those who are accustomed to the use of the word *love*, in Yorkshire, can interpret it very differently. For some people it is an expression of warmth and endearing, yet others could find it patronizing. In this chapter you will discover the sorts of words and phrases that are unlikely to draw good experiences to you. You will also discover techniques that will enable you to use words in a more affirmative way to create joyful and fulfilling experiences.

The use of certain words or phrases can be habitual. Sometimes we do not really think about what we are saying or why. These habits are also linked to social conventions about what is appropriate or not appropriate depending on the situation. To make changes to how you use words and phrases it is necessary to step back, to examine them and evaluate the sorts of experiences they draw to you. If you walk into your local shop and see a neighbor and they say, "How are you?" you may have a habit of giving a socially recognizable and habitual response such as, "Okay, thanks," "Not bad," or "Could be better." You do not really give the answer much thought as it is just a social lubricant to keep the conversation going. How often do you stop and consider how you are really feeling? What other possible answers could you give to the question? Perhaps you could respond with, "I'm feeling great," "I'm full of energy," or "I'm glad to be alive." It is possible, through practice, for you to change habitual responses and be more creative with your use of words and phrases.

It is not just the words that you speak or write that matter; your internal chatter is also important. Some people are highly aware of their internal chatter because it is experienced as a voice inside their head. This internal voice can encourage, discourage, criticize or support them. Imagine that you are in a team meeting at work and put forward a suggestion for improving the service provided to customers but your manager and co-workers do not appear enthusiastic about it. Your inner voice may then berate you with statements such as, "Why did I say that?" or "Next time I will just keep quiet." In some cases you can be your own worst critic. Constantly monitoring and blaming yourself does not result in good feelings and can often lead to destructive forms of behavior. If you are on a diet and then succumb to a large piece of chocolate cake your inner voice may pipe up, "I am so weak willed," "I cannot stick to this diet," or "I've blown this diet." With this type of internal dialogue you are likely to feel guilty and this can lead to a destructive cycle of starving and binging. After reading through the techniques in this chapter you will be able to start using creative and affirmative ways of using words both in relation to your internal chatter and your interactions with others. Be gentle and patient with yourself because changing our habitual vocabulary may take some practice.

The distinguished psychologist Albert Ellis has studied the use of words and found that certain words or phrases are particularly unconstructive including: don't, must, can't and should. As mentioned earlier in this book, the word *don't* can be unhelpful if it used to formulate changes in our lives because it focuses on what we do not want.

Here are some other examples of how we may use the word *don't* in everyday life:

Don't get **mad** at me	Don't make me **angry**
Don't **tell me what to do**	Don't **worry**
Don't **mention it**	Don't **forget**
Don't be **late**	Don't **do that again**
Don't be **afraid**	Don't **go there**

These examples focus on what you do not want, rather than what you do want. They emphasize getting mad, angry, being told what to do, worrying, mentioning something, forgetfulness or lateness. The phrase 'don't go there' has come into frequent use during the past few years to refer to things we would rather not talk about. If you are particularly bothered by an experience and someone tells you not to 'go there', then you may feel snubbed or that they have not really listened to you. Here are some ways of rephrasing these expressions in more affirmative ways.

Don't tell me what to do	**I am taking responsibility for my own actions**
Don't mention it	**You're welcome**
Don't forget the milk	**Remember to bring the milk**
Don't go there	**I feel sensitive about that issue**

Another way of turning around the unhelpful aspects of the word *don't* is to focus on what you could do instead.

Don't get mad at me – what could you do to keep calm?
Don't tell me what to do – what could you do to make this happen?
Don't be late – what could you do to ensure that you are on time
Don't do that again – what can you do differently next time?
Don't be afraid – what can you do to address your fears?

Exercise
Reflect upon the use of the word *don't*.
How often do you use it?
When other people use the word *don't* – how do you feel?
Rewrite some of the ways you use the word *don't* in a more affirmative way.

You might even be thinking, "I don't want to do this exercise," or "I don't believe it will work!" These phrases could be changed to, "This exercise will be enjoyable," or "Changing my words will bring more affirmative experiences to me." Experiment and find out which phrases result in more positive feelings.

Should

The word *should* especially if it is spoken with force sounds like a demand is placed upon you, rather than a request. You may have heard this word frequently at school, or in family situations. Your teachers, your parents or guardians could have used this word as a way of teaching you about social and cultural conventions and they can become a set of rules that you live by. I find it curious that when someone buys us a gift, we often respond "You shouldn't have." This suggests that we are rejecting the other person's kindness. Alternatively it could be that we have low self-worth and believe that we do not deserve a gift. Here are some examples of the use of the words *should* and *should not*:

- You should eat five fruit or vegetables a day
- You should stop smoking
- You should stop eating sugary snacks
- You should get a health check-up
- You should always send out birthday cards to family friends
- You should learn to drive
- You should get married
- You should have children
- You should tidy up
- You should go to the gym
- You should stop watching television
- You should go out more
- You should get a job
- You should get up early
- You should start a savings plan

The use of such phrases may be based on what appears to be sensible advice. Your partner may be concerned about your health so they want you to go for a check-up. Your partner's concerns may be expressed by saying that you should go to the doctor. Nonetheless by using the phrase 'you should' this sounds like a demand rather than a request. Some people resist or rebel against the demands that are placed upon them and may be less likely to do what is asked of them.

The flip side of should statements are should not statements. Here are some examples of the use of the phrase 'should not':

- You should not eat too much fried food
- You should not eat too many sweets
- You should not gossip
- You should not be selfish
- You should not spend so much money
- You should not work so hard
- You should not get up so late

- You should not watch so much television

Again these phrases are often based on what seems to be good advice, though they also sound like demands rather than requests. In these examples there is an emphasis on something that is deemed negative or unhelpful: fried food, sweets, gossiping, being selfish, overspending, working too hard, getting up late, or watching too much television. If you use the words should or should not, or you hear others using them, think about how they can be altered so that the emphasis is on choices or options rather than demands. For example:

- I could eat five fruit or vegetables a day
- I could stop smoking
- I could stop eating sugary snacks
- I can reduce my television viewing habits
- I could get up early
- I could go to university
- I could get a job

Because the emphasis is now on choice and options, you can also choose not to do something and yet phrase it in a positive way.

- I could get married, though I choose not to
- I could learn to drive, though at present I choose not to

Using the phrase 'have to' can also produce similar results to the use of should or should not. Saying that you have to do something can make this seem like a demand rather than something that you are choosing to do. Consider the following examples of 'having to':

- I have to stay late at work to keep up to my workload
- I have to buy my friend a birthday present

- I have to be positive no matter what
- I have to do all the exercises in this book
- I have to go to university
- I have to get a job

In these instances the phrase 'have to' can be challenged.

> Situation: 'I have to stay late at work, three nights per week.
> What can you do to keep up to your workload?
> What other options are available to you?
> What would help you reduce your workload?

Do you have to buy your friend a birthday present, or could you make a lavish card for them? Maybe you could treat them to a meal or a trip to the theatre or cinema. If you are short of cash you could make, rather than buy, your friend a present. You could bake a delicious birthday cake for them, or paint them a picture. If you think that you 'have to' be positive at all times then this can create tension because it is unrealistic. Life is full of ebbs and flows and there will be times when you feel more positive and at other times you may feel disheartened. Recognizing and accepting these ebbs and flows releases tension.

Exercise
Reflect upon the use of the words 'should', 'should not' and 'have to'.
How often do you use them?
Do these words seem like demands or requests to you?
Experiment with changing the word should for could – does this work better for you?

Using the word *could* rather than 'should', 'should not' and 'have to' opens up options and possibilities. There is also a difference in terms of commitment to change in using the words try, hope or will. If you say you will try to do something it tends to suggest that you are not fully convinced that you will do it or achieve your desired results. The word *hope* also contains a flicker of doubt. For instance, with a statement such as, "I hope I like this new job," there is a feeling of uncertainty behind it. Can you detect any differences between, "I will try to get a new car," "I hope to get a new car," or "I will get a new car"? Note also that the last statement is about action, of taking steps to obtain a new car. While there may be several steps involved and the process could take some time your commitment to obtaining the new car remains firm because this is something you will do, rather than try to do.

Similarly you may want to consider the differences between:

I am going to **try** to say no to taking on extra work at weekends

I **hope** that I do not take on extra work at weekends

I **will** say no to taking on extra work and working weekends

I am going to **try** to make an effort to meet people by joining a walking group

I **hope** to join a walking group to meet new people

I **will** join a walking group and meet new people

I am going to **try** to do the exercises in this book

I **hope** to do the exercises in this book

I **will** do the exercises in this book

After considering your choices and options you may want to make a firm commitment to something by using the word *will* rather than *try*.

I will go to the gym

I will get a health check-up

I will tidy up

I will reduce my television viewing

There are other words and expressions that can also generate negative ways of thinking, feeling and behavior including the use of the following:

What's wrong?	Problem	Impossible
Never	Always	

What's wrong?

When you think about what is wrong with something you may magnify these things and overlook what is right about them. For example, if you are and your partner are experiencing some challenges in your relationship you might start to think about what is going wrong. You might start to mentally catalogue the things that are wrong with the relationship such as: you are not spending much time together, your partner does not seem to listen to you or their habits are starting to annoy you. Thinking about what is wrong with the relationship can then bring about feelings of sadness, irritation or anger and you may start acting in a hostile way towards one another. On the other hand, if you shift the focus to the ways in which your partner is loving and supporting, such as buying small surprise gifts, helping you with shopping or washing the dishes each evening then you may feel more loving and cherish the relationship. Of course if there are serious difficulties in your relationship because your partner is violent or abusive, either mentally or physically, then it would be appropriate to find out what options are available to you in terms of protecting yourself or seeking out professional support.

Problem

Using the word *problem* can also be like a barrier that stops the generation of alternative ideas or actions. When you hear, "That is going to be a problem," or, "That is a problem," then you may feel discouraged and decide not to take any further action. For example, consider the following statement: "The problem with life coaching and using the law of attraction is it involves a lot of work doing exercises and making changes." Because this statement uses the word *problem* it is not inspiring, nor will it encourage the actions that will bring positive changes into your life. On the other hand, if the statement was changed to, "Life coaching using the law of attraction is challenging because it offers the opportunity to investigate and explore making changes in my life," this sounds more appealing. A challenge can be something that drives us, motivates us into action and leads to a sense of achievement. Reflect upon your own experiences: is there a difference, for you, between the use of the words *problem* and *challenge*? You could experiment with using the word *challenge* as a replacement for problem and see what changes this brings about. Alternatively the word *puzzle* can be substituted for *problem* so that it becomes a springboard for finding ways to solve it. Go ahead and test out different phrases and find out which are most effective for you.

Impossible

If we say that something is impossible then this closes down options and possibilities for change. Likewise other phrases such as, "That is never going to happen," can also be limiting, depending on the context in which they are used. If you are incredibly tall then you may say things like, "It is impossible to find clothes that fit properly." While it may be challenging to find clothing that fits you there are options that could be explored. You could search for on-line clothing manufacturers that specialize in clothing for tall people, find a dressmaker or tailor, form a group for tall people who have similar experiences where you could swap clothing or even have a go at making your own clothes. You may be interested in returning to studying as a mature student now that your children are growing up and yet say to yourself, "That is never going to happen," because I don't have the time, money or support to do so. Thinking this way will not attract positive change because it focuses on lack and limitation.

Always

The word *always* can be a sweeping statement that fixes something in place rather than opening up the possibility of change. Here are a few examples of how the word *always* can be limiting:

- I'm always getting things wrong
- I'm always in a rush
- I'm always spending too much
- I'm always eating junk food
- I'm always trying too hard
- I'm always doing things wrong
- I'm always overworking

When using the word *always*, pause and consider if this is the truth. Are there times when you get things right? Do you sometimes slow down and take things easy? Think of the times you resist spending money. Be honest, if there is a recurring pattern of behavior of making mistakes, rushing about, overspending or eating a lot of junk food. Acknowledging this is a way to start changing. On the other hand, are you are forgetting the occasions when you do act differently?

Never

The use of the word *never* can also be a way of denying options or choices that could lead to change. *Never* is a term that seems so final it closes the door to changes in the present and the future. If something will never change, or will never happen then you are not likely to pursue it. In this way you could be closing off the possibility of making positive changes in your life.

Here are a few examples of how the word never is used to describe life situations:

- I'll never get another job

- I'll never meet a suitable partner
- I'll never be rich
- I'll never lose weight
- I'll never stop smoking
- I'll never get on with my manager
- That will never happen
- I'll never learn to drive
- I'll never love again
- I'll never go to university
- I'll never get fit

Unhelpful combinations

The words *always* and *never* are sometimes used together making a potent mix, for example:

- I'm always eating junk food so I'll never lose weight
- I'm always overspending so I'll never be rich
- I'm always nervous on dates so I'll never meet a suitable partner
- I'm always in conflict with my manager so we will never get on

Additionally a range of unconstructive phrases can be strung together in a sentence, which may well make them seem stronger and fixed in place. Here are a few common examples:

My **problem** is **I can't** concentrate, I am **always** distracted so I will **never** be good at studying

My **problem** is I **can't** resist chocolate, I'm **always** snacking on chocolate bars so I'll **never** lose weight

My **problem** is I **can't** say no to other people. I am **always** taking on extra tasks so I **never** have enough time.

My **problem** is that I'm **always** oversleeping so I am **never** on time for work

Exercise

Consider the ways in which you might use such phrases in your everyday life and how you can rephrase them.

Identity and ownership

One of the most powerful uses of language concerns our identity and forms of ownership. Sometimes other people have used these expressions when talking about us and through force of habit we keep on using them. I was quiet and introverted as a child and was thought of as shy. Family and friends noticed the times when I was quiet and introverted and overlooked the occasions when I was more extroverted. Over time I started to internalize this identity statement and started to find evidence to support it, rather than refute it. Over time shyness could then become a part of my identity. Since then I have challenged the label of shyness that was attached to my personality and it is no longer true for me. This process took practice and occurred over many years. There is still a part of me that enjoys being quiet but at other times I can be more extroverted such as teaching larger classes at workshops, or at public speaking events.

Here are a few examples of limiting identity statements that maybe limiting your life experiences:

I am lazy	I am useless	I am too thin/fat
I am too old	I am too tall	I am too short
My lousy job	My back problem	My poor memory
My wrinkles	My bad moods	My unhappy relationship

Does laziness define your whole life? Is laziness something you want to claim as part of your identity? Who or what defines you as stupid? What are you good at? What are your unique talents and skills? If you think you are too short, what can you do to change this viewpoint? It is possible, for instance, to use clothes and fashion accessories to minimize or maximize your stature.

Likewise there are people who have become successful later in life. Susan Boyle was in her late forties when she became a global sensation after her appearance on a reality television show and now has a multi-platinum album to her name, which showcases her incredible voice. Using ownership phrases such as my lousy job can also be drawing un-supportive feelings and behaviors to yourself. Can you really own a job – or are you paid at this moment in time to fulfill a particular set of tasks and activities? If you go around talking about your poor memory, others might start to focus on this and point out the occasions when you have forgotten something. Subsequently you might get a reputation for having a poor memory and the whole thing becomes a self-fulfilling prophecy. If you do use ownership phrases, unpick them and question their accuracy.

- Sometimes I like to be lazy. At other times I work or play at full capacity.
- Although I may not be brilliant at math, I am really good at cooking delicious meals.
- A few wrinkles will not stop me enjoying life to the full.

Sometimes unhelpful words are strung together in a conversation.

Jack's Story
Jack was unaware of how he used negative phrases, and the sorts of thoughts, feelings and behaviors they attracted to him. During coaching Jack revealed that he had a habit of stringing negative phrases together. He reported that recently a good friend had asked him how things were going. Jack replied: "Everything is going wrong at the moment. My back problem is playing up. I hate my lousy job and I am too old to look for another one. I should see the doctor. I will try to re-arrange an appointment but the problem is I have too much

to do." Upon reflection Jack realized that these phrases were not likely to attract positive feelings or stimulate behavioral change. However, by questioning them, these negative phrases were unraveled. Using a step-by-step process Jack found that his comments to his friend were underpinned by magnification (everything is going wrong), identity labels that were not empowering (I am too old) and focusing on what he did not want (lack of time). Jack turned these phrases around by asking himself what was going right for him and the parts of his job that he did enjoy. He also thought about what he could do to delegate and re-arrange his time so that he could make an appointment with his doctor.

Metaphors

Metaphors are a way of creating a resemblance or contrast between different things. Sometimes a metaphor can generate stronger feelings than a literal description. It is useful to explore how metaphors are used and the sorts of feelings and behaviors they might be attracting to us. Paul, for example, dashed into a coaching meeting exclaiming, "Sorry I'm late. I was stuck in a traffic jam; it was a nightmare." He went on to say that while sitting in the lines of traffic he started to feel stressed and had a headache. Paul then said, "My head feels like a ten ton weight." By using these metaphors Paul was creating a likeness between the traffic and a nightmare, a headache and a large weight, both of which were not attracting good experiences. Another client, Amy, who came to coaching to overcome procrastination said that she was an expert in beating herself up about her poor time management. Through coaching we examined if this metaphor was likely to attract positive experiences to her and inspire her to change. Amy found that using this metaphor of beating was harsh and not supportive. Also the word beating suggested that she did not have the strength to overcome the challenge of better time management. It took some practice for Amy to cease thinking in this way because it had become habitual. Now Amy catches herself when she uses this metaphor and realizes that it is no longer true for her.

Metaphors may form part of a story that is used to describe our lives. Are you fired up with enthusiasm or feeling burnt out? Is life going smoothly or is it a bumpy ride? Are you willing to get into the driver's seat and move forwards in life, or are you looking in the rear view mirror? Are you soaring to great heights or are you down in the dumps? Perhaps you have a spring in your step. Do you feel that you are in the dark, or clueless? Or perhaps you regard life as an obstacle race that is full of hurdles. Maybe you are fuming or perhaps you are feeling chilled out.

Often metaphors are used with ownership phrases which makes them even more potent:

- My life is a disaster zone
- My life is shipwrecked
- My debt is like a stone round my neck
- My relationship with my partner is a minefield
- I have a sinking feeling about this new job
- I'm a self-confessed couch potato
- I have a mind like a sieve

The metaphors we use in relation to the body can also be limiting:

- I'm tearing my hair out
- I'm so wound up
- My spare tire
- My tree trunk legs

Other bodily metaphors can, however, be more positive. Maybe you have a swan-like neck or rosy cheeks. Metaphors which are inspirational are more likely to attract good experiences to us.

Metaphors that are based on nature, for example, can be a way of working through our experiences. Positive thoughts, for instance, can be regarded as seeds that are cultivated in our minds. Life itself can be thought of as part of a cycle of budding, blooming, decline and renewal.

Exercise

Consider some of the metaphors you use to describe your life (is life plain sailing, a bed of roses, or full of thorns?)
What sorts of feelings and behaviors do these metaphors attract?

Affirmations

Affirmations are positive statements that can be used as a way to reinforce new ways of thinking, feeling and behaving. They act as reminders because they are activated through repetition. Writing and repeating affirmations can be fun and can easily be incorporated into daily life. Affirmations can be written on small cards, sticky notes, or you could make a large poster to display them. Different colored cards, pens, paint, pencils or crayons can also be used to make the affirmations appealing to you. It is important to consider how to phrase affirmations so that they work effectively for you. There are also many helpful books that explain affirmations in more detail such as *Embracing Uncertainty* by Susan Jeffers or *I Can Do It: How to Use Affirmations to Change Your Life*, by Louise L. Hay, which you can refer to for further guidance. What follows are some step-by-step guidelines that you can use to formulate effective affirmations.

Feelings

The feelings or impetus behind your affirmations are incredibly important. If you just mechanically repeat the affirmations without really thinking about them, they will not be very effective. On the other hand, if you cultivate a really good feeling about your affirmations they will be more effective. One way of doing this is to imagine your affirmations are true for you and consider how they make you feel. If you are affirming that you are in the process of developing healthy eating habits, concentrate on how good this makes you feel, how much energy and vitality you have.

Personal

Affirmations are personal statements in which you declare what you want. It is the personalization of these statements that generates ownership and increases the feelings they produce. So affirming, "It is possible to make positive changes in life," is a positive statement but it lacks ownership. On the other hand, "I am now making positive changes in my life," makes the statement both positive and generates a sense of ownership. Also it is not possible to write affirmations to change other people since we cannot be held responsible for the changes that they make in life. Ultimately it is not possible to control another person's thoughts, so affirmations such as, "You will make positive changes in life," or "We will make positive changes in our lives," are beyond our control. Think of affirmations as a declaration of your responsibility and commitment to making positive changes in your life.

Positive

Affirmations are about attracting positive experiences rather than focusing on what you do not want. For example an affirmation such as, "I don't want to be lonely," is not likely to generate good feelings or attract a relationship to you. On the other hand, "I am increasing my social networks and meeting amazing new people," is more likely to inspire you and creates suitable conditions for new relationships to be formed. Similarly if you repeat, "I don't want to smoke anymore," it focuses on a habit that is not supporting your well-being. This can be rephrased to, "I have decided to have a smoke-free life."

Believable

For affirmations to be effective it is also necessary to write and declare affirmations that could be believable for you. If you are declaring, "I am gorgeous and everyone loves me," is this believable to you? A further difficulty with this affirmation is that your feelings about your appearance are related to how others respond to you. Is it realistic to expect everyone to love you? Increasing your self-belief and self-worth may be an incremental process. So a more practical affirmation might be, "I am in the process of making the most of my appearance." Similarly if you write affirmations that are untrue then they are not likely to attract positive changes into your life. So if you are repeating, "I am incredibly rich and financially secure," but have large credit card debts then this statement is untrue. The affirmation could, however, be rephrased to, "I am in the process of clearing my debts and improving my finances."

Present tense

Affirmations are effective when they are written and stated in the present tense. While you can change the ways you think about what has happened to you, the past has gone. Similarly if affirmations are written in the future tense then they remain out there rather than drawing them into the present. Affirmations that are future orientated can also distract you from making changes to your life at present. So if you affirm, "In two years' time I will achieve my ideal weight," then this focuses on a two-year timeframe and you may find that you are continually two years away from your desired weight. Some affirmations are a starting point for change and are phrased as, "I am in the process of." These can be inspirational and provide a catalyst for change. To be even more effective these need to be upheld with affirmations that focus on actions that will make your statements true for you.

Here is an example of how the timeline for affirmations can be used:

Perhaps you have made a commitment to improve your health.

1. You might start declaring, "I am in the process of learning more about being healthy."
2. When you have taken actions to improve your knowledge you may then write a further affirmation such as, "I am choosing to eat healthy foods," or "I am enjoying eating healthy foods."

Now that you have considered the different aspects of affirmations they can be mixed together to form positive life-enhancing statements. Here are some examples of positive affirmations for different aspects of life:

- My energy levels are becoming more stable
- I'm in the process of becoming fitter by taking regular exercise
- I am committed to taking regular exercise
- I am excited and energized about keeping fit
- I have decided to focus on abundance in my life
- I have decided to focus on my ideal work and how to achieve it
- I am attracting new clients to my business
- I am grateful for a loving and stable relationship

Affirmations can be displayed in many different ways. You could display your affirmations

- On the mirrors in your home
- The refrigerator door
- The front or back of your kitchen cupboards
- On your front wardrobe or chest of drawers
- In a picture frame

You could also write affirmations

- In a notebook and carry it in your bag,
- As a screensaver on your computer
- As text notes on your mobile telephone

After a while you may need to refresh your affirmations as your circumstances change. For example, if you have used affirmations about being in the process of applying for a new job and successfully achieve this then you can change your affirmations so that they focus on being effective and feeling fulfilled in your new role.

Regular practice
Affirmations work through regular practice. If you just say your affirmations once a day, or a few times a week it will take a long time for them to become new thinking patterns for you. However, if you practice the affirmations several times a day, on a daily basis, after about a month you will probably start to notice that you are thinking differently. I was surprised that after a month of regularly practicing affirmations that they started to become integrated into my thinking patterns. It was also easy to remember the affirmations at times when they were needed. For example, if I started to become aware of unhelpful feelings about lack of money I repeated affirmations that focused on gratitude for the abundance in my life. Now these affirmations have become a part of my subconscious and they are supporting new ways of thinking, feeling and behaving.

Exercise
Formulate some affirmations that are believable and will work for you. Here are a few starters:

I have
I am in the process of

I have decided to
I am grateful for

After reading the material in this chapter you can replace phrases, such as should, or should not, with phrases that focus on what you could do instead. You will also reinforce your commitment to change by replacing, what you hope to do with what you will do. In addition you could start to use positive inspirational metaphors to describe your experiences. During this chapter you have also learned to write your own affirmations using positive, present tense and personal language. The next step is to repeat your affirmations with feeling, on a regular basis.

Chapter Nine

Goal Setting

Positive thoughts, feelings and behaviors create the conditions for changing your life for the better but it is probably unwise to just sit around and expect good things to be attracted to you. Instead it is necessary to take action, to move towards your intended outcome. Once you take action you will be more likely to attract the positive life changes you desire. Goal setting is a powerful and effective way of making positive changes in your life. There are various aspects to goal setting that need to be taken into consideration so that they work effectively. Firstly setting goals involves making statements about your intentions and the outcomes that you will achieve. Secondly you need to specify how these outcomes will be achieved and set a time frame for their completion. During this chapter the goal setting process will be explained through a series of simple steps. When you start using these steps to formulate your own goals you will find that they help you to maintain your motivation and keep your positive changes on track.

There are differences between goals, dreams, fantasies and wishes. You may dream about winning the lottery but may not have worked out how to deal with such a large influx of money. You may fantasize about living on a lush tropical island without fully considering the climatic conditions. Wishes have a fairy tale quality to them, such as wishing that we could live happily ever after. Yet in an uncertain and complex world there are no guarantees that such wishes will come true. Dreams, fantasies, and wishes are valuable because they have an inspirational quality and you can tap into them and use them as a catalyst for taking action and making changes in your life. Yet for some people dreams may point to unresolved or psychologically disturbing issues. If this is the case then seeking the services of a suitably qualified counselor or psychologist can be helpful.

Some people are good at the goal setting stage but have difficulty achieving them. Just after a period of overeating you might make a resolution to go on a strict diet. Two weeks later your diet may seem too restrictive because you miss the enjoyment of eating your favorite foods and become less committed to your goal. It is more helpful to formulate a step-by-step process of goal setting that takes into consideration possible setbacks and the resources you can draw upon in such situations. By considering the possibility that a strict diet can become too restrictive you could explore ways of incorporating different foods, even your favorite ones, or treats into a long-term healthy eating strategy. You might also consider a range of resources that could help you to achieve the goal of long-term healthy eating habits such as joining a support group, finding a role model, or learning new cookery skills.

Goal setting is a structured way of planning how to achieve something in your life. Some goals are transactional because they are about obtaining specific skills or abilities, or changing a habit that is not supporting your best interests. Other goals are transformational because they have a deeper impact in your life. If your goal is to obtain another job then this would be a transactional goal. On the other hand if you want to find out your life purpose this would be a transformational goal.

Effective goal setting focuses upon outcomes that are within your control. If you were to set a goal to get the next job that you apply for, this is not something that is totally within your control. The interview panel may choose someone else who has more experience or qualifications. The organization concerned may decide not to appoint at all, or change the terms of the appointment. On the other hand, if you set a goal to develop your ability to be confident at your next interview, this is something that is within your control. There are several steps that you could take to be more confident such as practicing responding to questions with a life coach, or close friend, doing background research on the organization you are applying to, or learning more about body language.

Goal setting can be used to:

- Help you plan for your future, instead of just drifting along
- Turn ideas into an action plan so that you obtain your chosen outcome
- Increase your ability to take responsibility for decisions
- Allow you to record and reflect upon your achievements
- Enable you to make plans to improve your weaknesses
- Identify further learning, training or other development needs
- Help you to maintain a commitment to making positive changes in your life

However, there are some factors that can hinder the goal setting process including:

- Lack of interest in setting goals
- Thinking you are too busy
- It seems too complicated
- Lack of commitment to planning your future
- Not knowing where to start

It could be that you have come across goal setting in an organizational or sporting setting but are unsure how the same processes could be used in other areas of your life. While you may think that you are too busy, or that goal setting takes too much time, consider how much time and energy is wasted by just drifting along without a clear outcome in mind, or indulging in unhelpful habits. The journey towards your goal could be regarded as having equal importance to the final outcome because it involves growing and changing along the way. If you do not feel committed enough to start goal setting, it may be beneficial to return to the chapters on resistance or commitment in this book and revisit some of the exercises in those chapters. If you are not sure where to start then follow the step-by-step process outlined in this chapter so that goal setting becomes a manageable and achievable process for you.

10 steps to effective goal setting
1. Have a clear outcome
2. Outline the benefits of your chosen goal
3. Write down your goals
4. Set realistic and achievable outcomes
5. Set dates and create milestones
6. Consider the wider implications of your goal
7. Record the resources that will help you achieve your goal
8. Formulate a strategy for dealing with setbacks
9. Be flexible – revise, or change goals if necessary
10. Incorporate a reward for achieving your goal

Have a clear outcome

The first step in goal setting is to identify your intended outcome, in other words what do you want to achieve? Having a clear outcome is like having a defined destination in mind. For example, if you want to go to London, by train, you know where you are headed. If the train is diverted to another station, you will be able to make alternative plans to ensure that you reach your chosen destination. If you do not have a clear outcome, or direction, then you may easily become lost. Perhaps after completing the wheel of life exercise you have identified those areas you want to develop and change for the better. You then need to be very specific about the outcomes that you want to achieve in these areas. For example, perhaps you have identified time management as an issue you want to work on. If so, then consider what better time management means to you. Does this mean going to fewer meetings? Participating in at least one family outing each week, creating a roster for household duties thereby freeing up some more of your time? You might want to explore the following questions and write your answers down in a journal

- What is my intended outcome?
- What changes do I want to make?
- How can I formulate these changes into goals?
- What changes do I want to make on a short-term, medium and long-term basis?

Outline the benefits of your chosen goals

What will achieving your goals bring to you? What benefits will these goals bring into your life? How will these goals improve your relationships, family and working life? If you want to increase your fitness levels, then some of the beneficial aspects of this process could be having more energy, stamina and increased muscle tone. Remember that the benefits of the goal setting process relate to your thoughts, feelings and behaviors. These benefits do not depend solely upon external circumstances; it is how you respond to circumstances, situations and other people that is the important thing. One of the benefits of losing weight, for example, might be to raise your self-confidence. A further benefit could be that because your self-confidence has improved you are less likely to base your happiness or self-image upon what other people think or say about you.

Here is an example of a goal and the benefits it can bring:

Goal: To tidy up the family-home and reduce the clutter
Outcome: Tidier home, less clutter

Benefits:
- Ability to find things easily because they are in a specific place rather than just lying around the house;
- Creating more space by discarding things that are no longer used or in working order;
- A bit of extra money can be obtained by selling some of the things that are no longer wanted, at a car boot or garage sale, or on-line auction.

Exercise
Write down the benefits of achieving your goals in your journal.

Write down your goals

Writing down your goals makes them more tangible so you are more likely to be committed to them. If you just imagine the goals in your mind then you may forget them, or become distracted by other things. It is also incredibly motivating to record your actions and achievements. By writing your goals down in a journal or a word-processed document you can review them, revise them and return to them at a later date. You might want to write your goals on index cards and carry them around with you, so that you can refer to them frequently and reinforce your commitment to achieving them.

Set achievable and realistic goals

If a goal is too easy then there is no sense of accomplishment when you achieve it. On the other hand, if you set an unrealistic goal then this can be overwhelming. Reflect upon what is realistic and achievable for you, rather than focusing on what other people are able to achieve. Initially a goal may seem unrealistic but if you break it down into smaller steps then it could be more achievable. For example, it may be unrealistic to set a goal of running a marathon in three months' time if you have no prior experience of running, or have a health condition that might impair your fitness. On the other hand, if you set a goal of running in a shorter race in six months' time this may be more achievable. After achieving success in the shorter race, perhaps you would move onto developing further goals on running and over time you may even reach the stage where you could run a marathon.

Angela's Story

Angela made a decision to improve her fitness by running three times per week. She began by running for 5 minutes, then walking for 5 minutes, for a total of 20 minutes. She practiced this for a couple of days then increased her goal to running for 10 minutes, walking for 5 minutes and doing this for half an hour. Angela was very committed to her goal and purchased suitable clothes and training shoes. Angela was concerned about the ways in which her fitness plans might impact upon the time she spent with her partner. As a result she had a chat with her partner and they agreed to join her and keep fit themselves. Angela reported that her partner helped to sustain her motivation levels. Of course some setbacks did occur. Angela caught a flu virus during the winter months and this prevented her from her usual running routine. Nonetheless she returned to her goal because she had written it down and formed a commitment to it. Soon Angela was running for longer periods and noticed that she had become fitter. Angela became so enthusiastic about running that she signed up to do a charity race and set long-term plans to run a marathon.

Set dates and milestones

One way of developing your intended outcome is to set short-term, medium and long-term goals. By doing so you can make steady, incremental changes and feel a sense of accomplishment.

A short-term goal might be to find out about a new course in web design, a medium-term goal could be to apply for a course and the long-term goal would be to successfully complete the course. For longer-term goals it is also useful to create milestones along the way, to keep your motivation levels high. One of the milestones along the way to a web design qualification could be to successfully complete an assignment for the course. Without a sense of timing, goals become vague and your focus and motivation may dwindle. This can be detected in statements such as, "One of these days I would like to go to Australia for a holiday." There is an intention and stated outcome here, but there is no time scale. As a result there are no firm plans or list of actions that would result in going to Australia. On the other hand, dates and milestones can be set to make this intended outcome firmer and more achievable. Remember to make the time scales and milestones very specific. Rather than creating a goal to go to Australia in two years' time, you could state the month and year that you will go to Australia.

Consider the wider implications of your goal

Reflecting upon your values and the different roles you play in your life can help you to identify the wider implications of your goal. Think about how your goal relates to other people in your life, your finances, how you spend your time, perhaps even the ecological aspects of your intended outcome. For example, if your goal is to buy a larger car how might this impact upon you and your family? Would there be room for the car in your garage or driveway? How would this purchase impact upon the family finances? What about additional insurance or petrol costs for the larger vehicle? You might even consider the ecological aspects of running a larger vehicle in terms of petrol consumption and emissions. So when formulating your goal, spend time thinking about the benefits this will bring to yourself and those around you. If your goal brings benefits to you but this is at the expense of some other aspect of your life, such as relationships, finance or time, then some negotiating, compromising and reworking of your goal may be required.

Resources

There may be a range of resources that you can draw upon to reach your goals. These include books, television programs, on-line information, other people, experts, role models, time, commitment and energy. For example, if you set a goal of developing a long-term healthy eating strategy you could draw upon the following resources:

- Search the local library for books on healthy eating
- Watch cookery programs on television for recipe ideas
- Ask friends round for home cooked healthy food instead of eating out
- Create my own 'phone-a-friend craving helpline' to give you support when cravings for unhealthy food occur
- Ask friends for healthy eating tips, or recipes
- Visit a local health food store and ask about the products they have on sale

Writing down the resources that can help you achieve your goal will be beneficial because you can refer to it when setbacks occur, or when you start to feel de-motivated.

Setbacks

Experiencing setbacks is part of the adventurous journey you are making towards a more successful and fulfilling life. Sometimes setbacks can occur unexpectedly. Nonetheless how we overcome these challenges can be an incredibly enriching learning experience. Planning ahead and considering the possible setbacks that can occur as you move towards your goal can be extremely beneficial because it enables you to start planning how you would overcome them. Some setbacks maybe relatively minor, others could be more serious or potentially long lasting. Consider what you will do if you experience a health issue, changes to your financial situation or a change in your personal circumstances such as your relationships.

Be Flexible

Review your goals on a regular basis to check that they are still appropriate and the best means of obtaining your intended outcome. It is perfectly acceptable to revise, rewrite or set new goals when your circumstances or intentions have changed. It would be self-defeating to stick rigidly to goals that are no longer useful to you. Also it is better to revise or set new goals than simply discarding your old ones and giving up completely. The story below demonstrates the usefulness of flexibility in goal setting.

Monty's Story

Monty had been working on a family history project for three years and had tracked down family members in Poland, the United Kingdom and the United States of America. Monty was enthused by his success and decided to use a considerable amount of free air miles to return to the United States in order to follow up some new leads. However, Monty faced a setback when he experienced a heart condition, which resulted in staying in hospital for a couple of days. As a result of his heart condition he found it quite difficult to obtain health insurance. After much searching around Monty did find a company who would be willing to insure him but they wanted to charge a considerable fee, more than the cost the flight itself. As a result of these changing circumstances Monty decided to revise his goal of going to the United States. He realized that he could continue his investigations by returning to Poland and still use some of his air miles. When

Monty went to book a flight to Poland he found that the flights he wanted were completely booked up. Monty was now facing another setback but he managed to overcome it. He booked a flight to Munich and then took a train over the border into Poland. So while Monty did not achieve his original goal of going to the United States he did successfully complete his revised goal of going to Poland to do additional research.

If Monty had rigidly stuck to his original goal of going to the United States to continue his family history research he would have probably given up when circumstances changed. Instead of giving up, Monty revised his goal and was able to achieve this through a process of creative problem solving. In this way, Monty's story illustrates the importance of flexibility and adapting to changing circumstances.

Reward

When you achieve your goal remember to reward yourself; celebrate your success. Your reward could be something simple, yet meaningful, and it may not necessarily involve spending a great deal of money. There is a tendency to feel guilty or indulgent when rewarding ourselves, yet this is an important ritual which helps you to acknowledge your achievements, then move on to other adventures.

Ann's Story

One of Ann's short-term goals during life coaching was to switch from snacking on chocolate and crisps to healthier foods. Over the next few weeks Ann charted her progress. She started to eat cereal bars instead of chocolate especially during the afternoon, when her energy levels started to dip. As the weeks went by Ann found that she had started to lose weight and feel more energetic. When Ann met her goal she decided to treat herself to a trip to the cinema with her partner. Ann reported back that incorporating a reward into her goal setting helped her to maintain momentum and was also an enjoyable way to mark the positive change she had made to her eating habits.

Once you have achieved your goals it is important to formulate new ones, to keep you motivated. Sitting back after achieving your goal can in the long-term lead to stagnation. Perhaps you feel so good after achieving your goal, you are confident to attempt an even bigger goal for yourself.

In summary, writing down goals allows you to map out the changes you want to make in your life and when you will achieve them. Make sure that your goals are realistic and achievable. Write down your goals and refer to them often. Setting short, medium and long-term goals can help you to make incremental changes in your life. Most importantly remember to reward yourself when you achieve your goals. After you have achieved your goals, set some new inspirational ones.

Conclusions

During this book you have been invited to clarify what really matters in your life through reflecting upon your values, beliefs and the different roles that you play. Using tools such as the wheel of life you have started to raise your awareness of how the different parts of your life are interconnected. The wheel of life can, for instance, show how an imbalance in one area can reverberate into another area in your life. Low job satisfaction, for example, could have implications for your overall health and well-being. It is useful to revisit the wheel of life on a regular basis in order to map out how your life is changing through practicing some of the exercises in this book. Some life coaching clients find it helpful to revisit the wheel of life exercise on a monthly basis, others on a quarterly or annual basis.

The process of journal writing as a means of exploring and testing out the material presented in this book can also be a valuable and ongoing resource for you. Reading through your journal, you can track the changes you have made and the outcomes they have produced. Also, if you experience a setback or have a bout of negative thinking then your journal can be a source of comfort where you can express your feelings. Often the process of writing down your experiences can be healing. What you have written about can also provide a record of how you overcome challenges as you progress towards a more positive and fulfilling life.

Remind yourself that there are many different ways to define success. Some people might emphasize the material aspects of success such as the amount of money they earn, or the possessions they have accumulated. Others might equate success with establishing stable and loving relationships. Success might also involve several different dimensions, the material, the spiritual, as well as interpersonal relationships. By reflecting upon the exercises in this book you have the opportunity to produce your definition of success and what it means to you.

Even if you have read through the book, completed the exercises and started to put the tools and techniques it presents into practice, it will still provide a useful ongoing resource for you. It may be that you return to the book later, when specific changes occur in your life, such as a career change, new relationship or if a health issue crops up. Indeed after setting and achieving your first set of goals, you may return to the book with renewed enthusiasm to set even more life expanding goals for yourself.

There are several steps you can take to maintain the positive changes you have made in your life; here are a few suggestions. To begin with consider your relationships with colleagues, friends, acquaintances, neighbors and family. While some self-help books urge readers to discard negative people from their lives, this is somewhat impractical for several reasons. Firstly, there is no such thing as a purely negative person. There may be some underlying reason why a person thinks or behaves in the way they do. Secondly, it is not possible to live in a cocoon; you will come across people who exhibit negative thought patterns or behaviors at some point. By focusing upon your own thoughts, feelings and behaviors and the types of experiences they attract, rather than other people, you will be able to minimize the impact of other people's negative thoughts in your life.

Another aspect of maintaining a positive outlook relates to the books, music, films and television programs you engage with. Music can be a mood lifter. So you may want to compile your own playlist of feel good or motivational songs. Do you watch 'feel good', adventure or romantic films, or do you prefer thrillers? Dramatic violence has its place whereas graphic representations of mindless violence can be disturbing. The evening news on television helps us to be informed about what is happening in the world, yet there is often a heightened interest in disasters, fears, or tragedy. This can be balanced with other sources of information such as magazine articles, or books that provide more in-depth and nuanced representations of what is happening in the world. Reading biographies of inspirational figures can be incredibly motivating as they help you to reflect upon how someone overcame challenges or capitalized on opportunities. Spending time connecting to the natural world can also be an inspirational and healing experience. The wonderful colors of a sunset, the first spring flowers budding after a long winter, the sound of waves crashing on rocks, the dawn chorus of bird song are just a small part of the immense beauty of the natural world.

Above all consider that change is part of life, you will keep experiencing new things, so enjoy the process. Now that you have explored how to use your thoughts, feelings and behaviors so that they support your best interests, you will be better placed to attract positive changes into your life. Over the long-term you may find that positive attraction may manifest as being honest with yourself, listening to your inner voice, acting with integrity, keeping promises and expressing joy, gratitude and an inner sense of fulfillment.

Bibliography

Beck, A.T. (1976) *Cognitive Therapy and the Emotional Disorders*. New York: International Universities Press.

Beck, J.S. (1995) *Cognitive Therapy – Basics and Beyond*. New York: Guilford Publications.

Burns, D. (1999) *Feeling Good – The New Mood Therapy*. New York: Avon Books.

Byrne, R. (2006) *The Secret*. London: Simon and Schuster.

Dyer, W. (2009) *Stop the Excuses: How to Change Lifelong Thoughts*. London: Hay House UK.

Dyer, W. (2005) *You'll See It When You Believe It*. Arrow Books.

Hay, L. (2003) *I Can Do It: How to Use Affirmations to Change Your Life*. Carlsbad: Hay House.

Hicks, E. & J. (2007) *The Law of Attraction*. London: Hay House UK.

Jeffers, S. (2003) *Embracing Uncertainty*. London: Mobius.

Losier, M. (2009) *Law of Attraction – Getting More of What You Want and Less of What You Don't*. London: Mobius.

McFarlan, B. (2003*) Drop the Pink Elephant*. Capstone.

About the Author

Dr Melanie Chan has acquired knowledge, skills and experience of guiding both individuals and groups in positive life changes through a professional career in higher education and more recently through her life coaching company, MC coaching services. For over a decade Melanie has written course materials as well as publishing journal articles and book reviews. She has also presented personal and professional development seminars and workshops as well as speaking at conferences. Alongside the development of an academic career, Melanie is a certified life coach and NLP practioner who now runs a successful life coaching company.

BOOKS

O is a symbol of the world, of oneness and unity. In different cultures it also means the "eye," symbolizing knowledge and insight. We aim to publish books that are accessible, constructive and that challenge accepted opinion, both that of academia and the "moral majority."

Our books are available in all good English language bookstores worldwide. If you don't see the book on the shelves ask the bookstore to order it for you, quoting the ISBN number and title. Alternatively you can order online (all major online retail sites carry our titles) or contact the distributor in the relevant country, listed on the copyright page.

See our website **www.o-books.net** for a full list of over 500 titles, growing by 100 a year.

And tune in to myspiritradio.com for our book review radio show, hosted by June-Elleni Laine, where you can listen to the authors discussing their books.

mySpiritRadio